RUN TO THE BATTLE

A COMPILATION OF
THE INVADING FORCE,
A CALL TO ACTION, AND
RUN TO THE BATTLE

ROBERTS LIARDON

ALBURY PUBLISHING
Tulsa, Oklahoma

Run to the Battle
(A Compilation of *The Invading Force,*
A Call to Action, and *Run to the Battle*)
ISBN 1-88008-115-5
Copyright © 1999 by Roberts Liardon Ministries
P. O. Box 30710
Laguna Hills, California 92654

Published by ALBURY PUBLISHING
P. O. Box 470406
Tulsa, Oklahoma 74147-0406

Publisher's Note to This New Edition

This compilation of *The Invading Force, A Call to Action,* and *Run to the Battle* by Roberts Liardon will be a powerful addition to your Christian library and a vital source of inspiration and instruction for this last days' revival. No one doubts that we are living in extraordinary times which demand extraordinary spiritual discernment, wisdom, love, and faith. This volume delivers the divine mix of the prophetic and the practical. It will help every believer flourish as an extraordinary soldier for Jesus Christ in these last days.

The author has updated the original material in these works, but his prophetic voice still dominates the texts. The reader will find that many of the prophesies he made years ago when these books were written have already been fulfilled or are beginning to be fulfilled at the time of this printing.

We know you will be blessed by this latest offering of Roberts Liardon.

ALBURY PUBLISHING

TABLE OF CONTENTS

The Invading Force

ROBERTS LIARDON

Contents

Chapter 1

The Move Is On

They shall run like mighty men; they shall climb the wall like men of war; and they shall march every one on his ways, and they shall not break their ranks:

Neither shall one thrust another; they shall walk every one in his path: and when they fall upon the sword, they shall not be wounded.

They shall run to and fro in the city; they shall run upon the wall, they shall climb up upon the houses; they shall enter in at the windows like a thief.

The earth shall quake before them; the heavens shall tremble: the sun and the moon shall be dark, and the stars shall withdraw their shining:

And the Lord shall utter his voice before his army: for his camp is very great: for he is strong that executeth his word: for the day of the Lord is great and very terrible; and who can abide it?

Joel 2:7-11

I believe we are seeing the greatest outpouring of the Holy Spirit the world has ever experienced! This move of God is going to *invade* people's homes and communities. The prophet Joel was talking about an army, a force, that cannot be stopped. He talked about an army that does not break rank.

In taking a look at Joel's prophecy, how does today's army of God compare to this? Does the devil consider us to be an invading force and something to fear? The enemy should quake and tremble when you as a believer use the name of Jesus because when God's army — made up of you and me — invades, it wins.

In order to be part of this invading force, we must change our attitude toward God. We must line up our thinking with His thinking. As I travel across North America, speaking in both small and large churches, I see a great dividing line being drawn by the Spirit of the Lord. On one side stand those who are going on with the things of God, and on the other side are those Christians who are not moving with the Lord. An invading army must follow its leader, not follow their own whims and passions. An invading army is always advancing, not sitting around twiddling their toes. I want to be on the side of those who are going on with God.

Marching Orders

I believe that those who want to go on with God have to get vocal about their beliefs. They may have to "rock the boat," by stating their beliefs and standing by them. Those unwilling to move on with God may withdraw from you and say, "You are a fanatic! You are in error!" But you need to do what God tells you to do, and let everyone else be responsible for their own reactions or responses. Don't suffer any sleepless nights about what God tells you to do. Let those who don't like you or what you are doing have the sleepless nights.

If you have a vision from God you have not seen fulfilled yet, it is time for you to start exercising your faith for what God has promised you. As you keep invading, God will give you the faith to cause the whole vision to happen. Do not let other people hold you back. Keep marching and keep running because that is what God wants you to do in this day and hour. No matter what happens, if the call of God is upon your life and if God has given you a vision, concentrate totally on what He has called you to do.

People used to say to me, "Roberts, be very careful about what you say and do. You are young in the ministry. You do not have the higher education many other preachers do. You do not have a doctorate of theology."

For a while I listened to them, but the Word of God kept coming to me, and He gave me this second chapter of Joel. Notice that this army cannot be stopped and the soldiers have no fear. When people hear and see them they tremble in fear because this army is such a powerful force.

If you want to be part of such a force, God's end-time army of salvation, you must turn loose of the things that bind you. Loose yourself from words that hold you back. Be quick to obey the call of God.

Obeying God

We ought to obey God rather than men.

Acts 5:29

When God says, "Move!" don't discuss it — move! When God says, "Jump!" then jump! Too many believers want to discuss it. Some want to have a board meeting about it. Don't do that. When God says, "Get up and go," then get up and go. Don't ask questions — just go! When you get to your destination, God will take care of everything.

Trust in the Lord with all thine heart; and lean not unto thine own understanding.

In all thy ways acknowledge him, and he shall direct thy paths.

Be not wise in thine own eyes: fear the Lord, and depart from evil.

Proverbs 3:5-7

God is not going to use people who are too busy asking questions. He wants to use people who are established in the Holy Spirit. He doesn't want to use people who feel they need to hold a board meeting about everything. God uses people who hear, trust, and obey Him. He wants an army of believers that does not understand the word no. The only thing they are concerned with is God saying, "Go," so they can go and experience victory every time God sends them!

Look at Abraham. God said, "Abraham, get up from this country and go over there." (See Genesis 12:1.) Abraham did not know where "there" was, but he got up and left Ur of the Chaldees. He did not sit around and ask the city council what they thought about God's instructions. Abraham just left for "there." That is what you need to do when you hear from God. Do not let anything hold you back. Do not let religious circles hold you back from flowing with God's Spirit.

The reason so many churches start in the power of the Holy Spirit and then collapse is because they try to put the Spirit of God in a box. They want the move of God to be so organized that it fits in with their schedule and follows their agenda. There is nothing wrong with organization, and we are to do everything decently and in order, but we also need to be flexible enough to flow with the Spirit of God. (See 1 Corinthians 14:40.) Never tell the Holy Spirit what to do — He tells you what to do.

> He who dwells in the shelter of the Most High will abide in the shadow of the Almighty.
>
> I will say to the Lord, "My refuge and my fortress, my God, in whom I trust!"
>
> **Psalm 91:1-2** NASB

When we are dwelling in the shelter of Almighty God, we are constantly in His presence. Believers are to abide in the shadow of the Almighty. When God speaks, we should obey simply because He is God and we trust Him. Do not question what God says, and do not worry about what other people are going to think about it. Just obey!

Losing the Fear of Man

For a long time, the Lord told me to use my little book, *I Saw Heaven*, as an evangelistic tool. He told me to get it into as many places as I possibly could as fast as I could. I said, "God, that is a wild story to some people. Even though it contains scriptures, it is almost controversial. Some religious people do not like it, especially when they know I am quite young and inexperienced. God, why don't we hold off?" My greatest fears were that people were going to say I was in the ministry just for the money, or that they were going to accuse me of building my ministry on my testimony of going to heaven. But I knew in my heart those criticisms were not true.

God replied, "Don't you dare. You have got to do it! You do not need to be ashamed of what God has given you. You have got to be a power — a force."

Then the Lord spoke to me through a woman evangelist. As we were having dinner one night, she looked up and said, "Roberts, today God gave me something for you. God has been speaking to me to get my literature into the hands of as many people as I can, as quickly as I can. I was looking through some magazines, and I saw your advertisement in one. When I saw it, the Spirit of God told me that I need to advertise too. And this is what He told me to tell you. He said, 'Anytime I have given you a truth or moved in your life and have told you to give it to the people, you should not be ashamed of it. You should use every avenue to get it into the hands of people, even if you have to force it into their hands!'" I finally got rid of all the fears of what people might think of me when my book began to be translated into different languages.

Reaching beyond your own community into the uttermost parts of the earth is a mark of this end-time move. If you are always invading and conquering lands, what your critics say will not amount to anything. By the time they start speaking against you, you will have doubled your outreach and gone on to something else.

Understand that we live in a critical point in time. The world is coming to an end, time is coming to a close, and the last voice must be the voice of God to the lost of this world. No longer will there be a few superstars. There will always be those in the traveling ministry, but local churches — large and small — will be used mightily in this end-time move of God's Spirit.

Pastors, never be satisfied. Always look for new horizons. Always keep invading. Always be doing something. Do not let the enemy stand in your way. Cause the devil to fear. Reach out to the ungodly and let your church be known for its compassion and outreaches. Do not fear what people say. Let them fear you.

Spiritual Strategies

The Lord also told me, "Roberts, preach what I give you, no matter how 'far out' it may sound."

If you are familiar with my ministry, you know that I do preach what some think are "far out" sermons because I know there is another world that most people have not experienced yet. There is a realm in the spirit where you can walk, talk, and live. By the sovereignty of God, I believe a few people have tapped into that realm once in a great while, but not many people want to live in it.

People do not know how to get to this realm in the spirit, and when you start preaching about these things, it rocks the boat — especially the devil's boat. Satan does not want people to invade his demonic world. He prefers to invade our world instead. He always wants to be on the offensive, but it's time for us to be on the offensive. We need to invade Satan's territory. We need to put fear in his heart.

When you invade, it causes faith to grow in your heart, power to come into you, and tells God that you are going to move on with Him. I do not have much patience with people who are always "waiting on their ministry." When I get around Bible school students in particular, I do everything I can to get them to do something, even if it is not along the lines of their ultimate calling.

"Just do something," I tell them. "Go witness on the streets. Visit people in the hospitals. Start invading. Do not sit and wait for a vision from God. Do not wait for someone else to hear for you. If God tells you to do something, do it! Keep the fire burning in your heart. Continue to seek new heights. Don't retreat. Attack! Always be an aggressor. Always go forward. Be a part of God's great army."

This aggressive attitude is what Joel prophesied about. He said that in the last days, there would arise young men and women and old men and old women who would move in power under the mighty hand of God's Spirit. (See Joel 2:28.) These men and women of God will not be defending the city; they will be invading the city.

We need to be out where life is real. Yes, there's a time to lock ourselves up in our prayer closets, but we have a real life to live. We have a work to do for the kingdom of God. Many Christians do not know what it is to be in a battle. They do not know what it is to attack the forces of the devil. They only know what it is to defend, and defending is not fun. Attacking is fun. When we learn to attack, we learn one of the joys of being a Christian. If we are always defending, life gets tough. We get tired and we want to quit and go someplace else.

And let us not be weary in well doing: for in due season we shall reap, if we faint not.

Galatians 6:9

Great preachers like Smith Wigglesworth are always attacking and invading the devil's kingdom. It is fun when you are the one who starts the battle. It's similar to a sporting event. You can't win without a good offense. You can have the best defense in the world, but if you don't have anyone who can run the ball down the field or put the ball in the hoop, you'll never win. It is fun to win!

To win, you must learn spiritual strategies to use in surprise attacks against the enemy. You must learn to go to the throne of God. You must learn how God operates in the realm of the spirit, and you must learn how to flow and work with the angels of God. I am not talking about something imaginary. I am talking about a realm that is very real, and it is in and around us today. Sadly, many Christians do not know about this realm or else they ignore it.

Do not hold back those who are going on into this realm. Whether you understand spiritual warfare or not, don't dare speak out against those who are in the invading force. God protects those who are obedient to Him. Believe me, in this day and time, God's hand is going to protect His people. When you win a victory in the spirit world, you will have victory in the natural world.

You must learn to walk in faith to be in God's invading force. You can hear all kinds of faith formulas and other good teachings on faith, but there is another realm of faith that you cannot define. That realm must be experienced, and you must learn to walk in it.

People often ask, "How do you do such things? Why do you say such things? Where is that place? Can you tell us about it?"

I really cannot. All I can say is, "I know it is there, but you have to get in it and you have to live in it to know what it is like. I can only help you build a foundation. I am trying to impart to you that fire, that zeal, that strength, and that knowing that is within my heart, so you can rise up, invade the powers of darkness of this world, and control them with God's wisdom."

That is what God has called you to do. He wants you to rule the money of your city. He wants you to rule the political system of your city. He wants you to rule in every area of your life. If you begin to invade the realm of the spirit in your area, you will come against the "principalities and powers," some of the most powerful forces of darkness in the earth today, not just lesser demons. Principalities and powers are strong and they are smart. But God is bigger, and He is smarter!

Unlimited Power

The earth must know where Christians stand. The devil must know who we are and that we have power because the day is coming when the prince of the powers of darkness is going to stand on one side of a stage and God's people are going to stand on the other. We better know we have power through our Creator. We'd better know that when we speak, God is going to move.

The powers of darkness are going to be able to perform signs and wonders. (See 2 Thessalonians 2:9.) They are going to be able to do unusual things, so we must have God's power to control them. We have to be a force with unlimited power. Most Christians today, like Samson, know the limits of their power. We must get to the place where we know no limits, and where we know that *all* power is given unto us.

This power is available and we can walk in the realm of the spirit. Many people, however, are trying to use formulas to achieve this power. There is nothing wrong with sermons that give steps to success, but you cannot give step one, two, and three to get to the place I am talking about. It is different for every person. Every responsibility is different, but whatever it costs and whatever it takes, it is worth it. Give up all and seek the kingdom of God. Give up all to do His good work.

We are coming to a critical time in the realm of the spirit and in the world. This age is coming to a close, and we need to be busy invading. We have to let the earth know there is a God and He is alive and well. The only way this is going to happen is when enough people declare, "I know God reigns. See this?" BAM — there is a miracle.

We need the power of God flowing in our lives. Power is what we need, not just talk. The power of God is available to every believer. God has no favorites. The only reason there are superstars in God's work is because so few people are willing to pay the price to get there. What God gave to some people in the Bible and down through history is available to us today if we will pay that price. The great believers of the past were people who invaded. They knew how to work with angels, and they surrounded themselves with people who had that same spirit of invading.

Joshua was looking ahead — always planning the invasion. If you have a Joshua as a pastor, get behind him and join him in the battle. Never speak against him. Always pray for him. One of the main reasons churches fall is that when God begins to move, the devil encourages some of the members to criticize what the pastor is doing. Of course, they do not realize it is the devil. They think those critical thoughts are their own, and they receive them and act on them. Don't be guilty of this!

When a pastor first starts a church, he will make mistakes. When you criticize him, you give the enemy ammunition. The devil hears and acts on the words you say, just as God acts on what you say. Do not say, "The pastor is going to fail." That gives the devil another degree of power to use against the church. Instead, go home, get in your prayer closet, and say, "God, if I am wrong, change me. If my pastor is wrong, change him. But do whatever is necessary to make this church to succeed for Your glory."

Be careful what you do and say. Follow the leading of the Holy Spirit, do what the Bible says, and put your whole heart in it. (See Colossians 3:23.) Do not try to change things to fit the way you believe. Do not speak out against any man or woman. Walking in divine love will cause the power of God to come, and that will prove to men that you are real.

God's power is not going to come to a person who is playing games and doing what he wants to do. His power is going to come to those walking according to His laws. The New Testament has laws and regulations in it as well as the Old Testament. Many people say, "But we are under grace. We can do anything we want to do." That is what you think! God says we are to walk in love, but how many do this? God gave us certain commandments and He did not add, "If you want to, walk in love." No, He said, "Do it!" So many people do not want to do what God says. They want to play games and do what they want to do.

To be part of God's army in these last days, you must obey His laws and rules without question. You must walk in them with all your power and might. This does not take great faith. You can have a small amount of faith, add hope to it, direct it to the throne of God, and He will take it and use it to your benefit.

Many Christians are trying to achieve things in their own strength. They want to be gold or silver vessels when God simply is looking for yielded vessels. That is what you must be. You do not need a college education to serve God. You do not need to be wealthy to serve God. Those things are nice, and God may call you to pursue them, but with or without worldly goods and knowledge, to serve God means being a yielded vessel.

Others may try to discourage you by saying, "You don't know this and you don't have that. You have only been a Christian for a short time." But I'm telling you, God is not looking at all those things. He is looking for yieldedness, the obedience of your heart. If you can learn to live in a state of yieldedness to the Holy Spirit, you can accomplish great

things for God. One of the greatest secrets of the kingdom of
God is learning to yield to the Holy Spirit.

Chapter 2

Summoned to His Great Army

We are being called, or summoned, to be part of a great army that cannot be stopped. We are to run like mighty men. We are to hide the Word of God in our heart as our strength. When people go to war, they know the possibility is great that they will face tragedy or death. But when we become a part of God's invading force, we will not be hurt. We will always be protected, and we will bring fear to the camp of the enemy.

> **No weapon that is formed against thee shall prosper; and every tongue that shall rise against thee in judgment thou shalt condemn. This is the heritage of the servants of the Lord, and their righteousness is of me, saith the Lord.**
>
> **Isaiah 54:17**

No wonder worldly people fight those who are going on with God. It causes the demons in them to scream and quake. Demons know when we walk down the street if we have power. The presence of

Jesus in us should cause them to scream and come out of people. That is the way it should be, and it is possible to achieve this. You can have this power, but it is up to you to get it. It's not just for special people or for those who do special things. You just do what God tells you to do, and the Holy Spirit will empower you.

When Jesus walked up to a man who had a legion of demons in him, those demons knew who Jesus was. They said, "Son of God, why have You come here to torment us?" (See Mark 5:7.) That is the way it should be with all Christians.

Many are tired of hearing that Jesus is coming soon because generation after generation has heard this since He went back to heaven. Many people alive now have heard that message for fifty years. They have almost given up faith and hope, but He is coming soon! Do not ever lose that hope. Keep it within your heart. Let there always be a knowing within you that God's power and glory are coming. Jesus is coming soon, and we will be leaving this world. In the meantime, we have to be a force, a power that cannot be stopped or quenched. We must be a power that is always going forward and never resting. There is no time to rest.

God's army doesn't relax and take vacations when it comes to doing His work. You personally may take time off to relax and time for a vacation, but never let a day go by that you do not spend time in His Word and seek His face. Even on vacation, you may find yourself witnessing to people or casting demons out of someone. God is going to do the unusual in this day and time! Isaiah talks about the strange acts of God (see Isaiah 28:21), and I am longing to see them. We have seen a few acts of God, but I don't believe we have seen anything yet. Our eyes will behold the mighty outpouring of God's Spirit.

No matter how large your church may become, remember that it is the members who carry the church, not the guest speakers. It is *you* who must become the invading force. The fivefold ministry gifts are the leaders of God's end-time army. They visit your church, give the orders, and exhort the troops. Then they move on to another camp and do the same thing. It is the troops, however, who must carry out those orders and do the actual invading. We all must go where the light is dim, the Gospel is not heard, and the power is not known.

God said to me once, "While you are young, you are going to go to all the rough places."

I replied, "I don't want to go there. I want to go to Europe where it's nice."

He said, "You are not going there until you get old."

I said, "Well, that's nice. Your mercy endureth forever, Lord."

And He said, "Yes, it does."

Most of my overseas invitations are from rough places. They are always from the third world countries on the brink of war! But when you are friends with God, you can talk to

Him about anything — even the rough places — and He understands what you mean. He is my Friend. He lives with me, walks with me, and talks with me. I know what He likes and what He dislikes, and He knows my heart. I can look up to heaven and say anything, and He will just smile at me. I have never offended Him by joking with Him.

Many people misunderstand this statement because they are using *common* sense instead of listening to their spirit. In other words, to understand God you have to get over into the world of the spirit. That is one reason God is going to use young people in this new move — they do not have *common* sense. They do not understand the word *no*, they only understand go. They are going to run in the glory of God. They are going to go to presidents and kings and say, "Thus saith the Lord ..." and see changes take place in the nations.

God is moving. God is creating more visions. God is speaking to His people as never before. We need to open our ears and hear what He is saying, and then move to perform it, not sit back and discuss it. Once you are certain the voice speaking is God, discussion would be of the devil. If God says, "Jump through that wall," and there is no hole there, just start jumping. By the time you hit the wall, there will be a hole there. It is God's business to put the hole there. Your business is to obey, step out in faith, and start jumping. That is invading. That is where we need to be.

The Balanced Walk

There must be a balance to everything we hear. We must be able to operate with discernment because as soon as God speaks the devil is also going to speak. Satan will try to deceive us any way he can. However, if we are led by the Holy Spirit, we will not fall into error. Jesus said that the Holy Spirit will guide us into *all* truth, not *partial* truth. (See John 16:13.) To stay balanced, we must make sure our hearts are clean, our lives are pure, and our motives are right. The Holy Spirit **will reprove the world of sin, and of righteousness, and of judgment** (John 16:8).

I believe the day will come when believers will operate with such sensitivity to the Holy Spirit that there will not be as many mistakes. There will be perfection. When there is no error and there is only a hunger and a thirst after God, the Spirit of God will fall upon us in a greater way than we have ever seen. He will move in our hearts and give us what we desire.

There is more to the Christian life than what most people think. After we are saved, we have a battle to fight. We have a war to win, and we are in it whether we want to be or not. As soon as we are born again, we go into boot camp just like the young men of modern-day Israel. However, many Christians deliberately try to flunk boot camp. They do not want to fight. They want to stay where it is easy, so they end up defending the camp.

Learning to attack is a lot more fun because God needs no defense. He is His own defense. He needs people to attack the enemy for Him. He wants you to go forth and conquer, to be a voice, to carry a standard for Him, to say, "This is the way it is going to be," and then to have the power to perform it.

God's power cannot be unlimited in this world until we learn to do what He says, prove to Him we are real, until we walk the floor in prayer, pay our tithes, pray for the sick, and witness to the lost — even if no one is saved or healed. Most people do not want to do that. When they pray for the sick, they want everyone to be healed. Even if it does not happen every time, you have to keep on praying. That is called invading.

When you invade, do not have second thoughts and retreat — just invade. You are in it to the death — not your death, but the devil's death. Your attitude needs to be, *I am going to win, or I am going to die fighting.*

Not that I have already obtained all this, or have already been made perfect, but I press on to take hold of that for which Christ Jesus took hold of me.

Brothers, I do not consider myself yet to have taken hold of it. But one thing I do: Forgetting what is behind and straining toward what is ahead,

I press on toward the goal to win the prize for which God has called me heavenward in Christ Jesus.

Philippians 3:12-14 NIV

Spiritual Violence

And from the days of John the Baptist until now the kingdom of heaven suffereth violence, and the violent take it by force.

Matthew 11:12

Violent people do not have *common* sense. When people are violent enough, they always win. When we think of violence, however, we usually think of criminal activity or something that is wrong. But if we get violent for God and use this spiritual violence as a positive force, we will build our churches. We will build our television stations. We will own our own satellites. We will own land. We will just invade the whole place. We will set captives free, heal the sick, and take our authority back from Satan. That is the way it should be. Until end-time prophecy is fulfilled, let us rule over the forces of darkness through the name of Jesus. Let us be a power. Let us be a force!

If you do not want to go on with God, then go home because you are going to get upset with those who are doing something. I would rather not hear you complain because you may be judged. The first thing God usually does in a church when someone speaks out against what He is doing is remove them. He will deal with them in mercy first, then He will deal with them in judgment. He will remove them because this army must be a strong army to succeed.

Too often, we are afraid of what people are going to think if we stand up and proclaim God's Good News. For some, it's not worth it. But for those who want to invade Satan's dominion, it doesn't matter what people think. Let them worry about it. Let them have the sleepless nights. You shout the victory. You shout up and down the aisles of the churches. Let the earth know who God is by performing miracles and proclaiming Him on the streets. Give the people truth. Don't hold back. Give it everything you have. Invade the world of darkness with all your might, and take back what belongs to you.

If you are in poverty, get violent about it and learn how God wants you to prosper so you can give more into His kingdom. Enjoy prosperity and let your critics cope with it. If you are sick, get violent about it, and curse the sickness. If other sick people get upset because you are well, let them keep their sicknesses. One day they will wake up and want to be like you. After they decide they want to get rid of all the demons that are causing their sickness, they will come to you and ask, "Please teach me how to do it." Believe me, they will.

If you want power from God, ask the Holy Spirit to empower you. Let those who do not like it cope with it. Just watch them. They will eventually come back to you and say, "Teach me, teach me!"

When I first began in ministry, no one thought I would make it because I was so young, but I am still here. They are still coming to see me, but now they are saying, "Teach me, teach me." I say, "Yield," but they do not understand.

The simplest things sometimes are the most complex for believers to understand. God is simple and the things of the Lord are so simple that most people miss them. It is so simple to get the gifts of the Holy Spirit. You do not have to achieve anything — just yield. "Yield" is a simple word and a simple action. Allow God to fill you up and give you everything He has for you. Be obedient to Him and His Word. That is being a yielded person. Give the glory to God and have fun.

The Christian walk and the witnessing that belong to the Christian lifestyle are easy when you are attacking and obeying. Things get difficult if you are just defending and not attacking. I have noticed that some people witness in a defensive manner. If they are talking to someone who is not Spirit-filled, they defend tongues. Forget about defending — just proclaim the baptism of the Holy Spirit as a truth and let them find it. Do not give a definition to everything you do. Don't apologize for the works of God. Get free from that bondage and let other people cope with their own beliefs. Just do what needs to be done.

Why Be Prosperous?

The earth shall quake before them; the heavens shall tremble: the sun and the moon shall be dark, and the stars shall withdraw their shining:

And the Lord shall utter his voice before his army: for his camp is very great: for he is strong that executeth his word: for the day of the Lord is great and very terrible; and who can abide it?...

And I will restore to you the years that the locust hath eaten, the cankerworm, and the caterpillar, and the palmerworm, my great army which I sent among you.

And ye shall eat in plenty, and be satisfied, and praise the name of the Lord your God.

Joel 2:10-11,25-26

That is for you and me. No longer will the Church have needs that are not met. I believe the day will come when we will be multi-million-dollar organizations with enough money to buy anything we want and to invent anything we need. It is going to come to that, so if you do not like a church that's rich, go find a poor one. We see in this second chapter of Joel that the Lord promises to bless us, and we will eat in plenty.

We are moving into the most prosperous time the Christian army has ever seen because we are beginning to win. We are beginning to understand what belongs to us. Let those who are bound with religious tradition have their tradition. Let them live in their poverty, and let them enjoy their demons — if they can. As for me, I am going to enjoy all that the Lord has for me. **Forget not all his benefits**

(Psalm 103:2). Most people reject God's benefits when they arrive at the door. They say, "I don't want them." Well, send them to me!

Many ministers worry that if they start invading or start doing something out of the ordinary, their support will crumble, their popularity will disappear, and people will speak out against them. Yes, those things can happen if you start going with God. The financial support that was promised to you from the natural may fall away, but you must remember that God is your Source.

Evangelist Oral Roberts said, "God is your Source" so many times over television that people may not really hear it anymore. Nevertheless, it is true. You must understand that God is your Source. We look not unto man but unto God, who is our Source, our Creator, our Provider, and the One we call upon in the time of trouble. We ask of Him and we receive. God has a million people He can move upon to get our needs met. We do not need to worry. We need to have faith in God. Do not doubt God, and do not worry.

Peace I leave with you, my peace I give unto you: not as the world giveth, give I unto you. Let not your heart be troubled, neither let it be afraid.

John 14:27

Do not let your checkbook hold you back. If you cannot give of your finances, then mow the church lawn or help clean the church building. Do *something*. Start somewhere. When we think "offering," we usually think of money. Now, money is important. It takes money to spread the Gospel to every creature, and it has got to come from this army. But giving money is not the only thing you can offer God. You have talents and abilities that have been placed inside of you by God — use them for His glory and for His kingdom!

A lot of people think, "If I can't give $1,000, I am not going to give." You have to start somewhere. Give whatever you can. If you think you are poor, you should see the Africans to whom I preach. They live in little huts with one light — a string with a light bulb. The holes in their roads are the size of a car. People are dying in Africa, and their families are being massacred by the new armies taking over in many countries. The people are not allowed to own anything anymore.

I decided to teach them how to prosper, and the devil ran true to form — he sent a negative thought before I could preach a positive one. He said, "They do not have anything to give. Prosperity does not work here in Africa."

I said, "Devil, that is a lie!"

So I began to teach the Africans, "If you do not have anything, if you cannot bring food to the pastor to give to the needy, then get a rock. Get a plant. Get a leaf. Get something! Do something for the church. Knit socks for the pastor's son. Paint a picture, even if it is ugly, and hang it up somewhere.

Do something. Let God know you are real. Let the devil know you have faith in God. Tell all of heaven, earth, and hell that you are going on with a great God. You have to do something now. You cannot always wait for your day of prosperity to dawn. Help it dawn. Cause it to dawn."

So the Africans got their rocks and started polishing them. They began bringing things to church. They brought me a mat and said, "You can put it by your bed, and you can kneel down on it." They started to do something. They did not ask questions, they just moved. That is where Africans have it over Americans. Their situation is so critical that if they do not do something, they will die.

Walking by Faith

It is time to get back to the simple things of God. So many people want new revelations, and believe me, we will get new revelations because God enjoys enlightening our eyes. But remember, no matter how many revelations you get on faith — faith is still faith. It is not complicated. Just believe in the Creator. Learn to rely on unseen resources. Learn to reach and grab something you cannot feel. Learn to walk where there is no ground. Learn to accept victory when it seems there is no victory. Learn to rely on an unseen Person. That is faith!

Many of you stand on the threshold of taking the first step toward fulfilling the vision God has given you, but you have things in your lives that the devil is trying to use against you — family problems, social problems, emotional problems, or financial problems. God says, "Have faith in Me because I will help you. I know what I am doing better than you do. I know what is going on. My eyes go to and fro throughout the earth. They see everything. My hand is all-powerful. It knows no limits."

Freedom From the Past

God is willing to work with you if you will have faith in Him. Do not let your heart be troubled. Have faith in God. Ask for forgiveness for those things that were problems for you in the past. Let them go into the sea of God's forgetfulness, and once they are forgiven do not dig them back up.

Do not allow the enemy to torment you with something God has already forgiven you of. If the devil tries to throw it back in your face, invade his territory, attack him, and say, "No! My sins are gone forever. I am free because of the blood of Jesus Christ." Hit the devil with chapter and verse from the Bible. Be free in the glory and the Spirit of God.

If we confess our sins, he is faithful and just to forgive us our sins, and to cleanse us from all unrighteousness.

1 John 1:9

It is vital that no matter what your past was like, you realize you have been forgiven. If you have problems, God is the Answer. God is the great I Am. He is the God of the now. He cares for you. He loves you. If you have been through a divorce, if you have claimed bankruptcy, if you were in sin — no matter what happened — God's grace is almighty. Jesus' blood cleanses us from all sin. When you say, "God, forgive me," He is quick to forgive you. He says in His Word, **Before [you] call, I will answer** (Isaiah 65:24). Believe me, He is just like that! He is a God of His Word.

Forget the past. Look up and see new horizons. See your destiny from God's viewpoint. Do not look at what is behind you. That is the reason the Spirit of God told the apostle Paul to write these words: **I press toward the mark for the prize of the high calling of God in Christ Jesus** (Philippians 3:14). The Holy Spirit did not call it the *low* calling, but the *high* calling. If it is a high calling, you have to look up. Forgetting everything that is behind you and in the past, look forward, press on! That is what God has planned for you.

The Invading Force

Jesus invaded. The apostle Paul invaded. The disciples and the apostles invaded. When the apostles came to town, the people said, "Oh, no! Here come those men who have turned the world upside down" (See Acts 17:6.) Can that be said of us? Is today's body of Christ turning the world upside down? We should be even greater than the early church.

I was once ministering in Missouri with a certain prophet of God. We visited a very good church, but the pastor was extremely cautious. The bigger the church gets, the more cautious the pastor needs to be. I can understand that, and I believe that is of God, but the Spirit of God led us to that church. We did not know they did not believe that Christians can have demons.

Demons can enter your mind and your body, but if you are a Christian they cannot enter your spirit. If they oppress your mind, they will cramp your spirit. You need to be set free, and you need someone to help you get set free.

I was preaching in this church and the Spirit of God said, "Give a call for deliverance." About a thousand people were there and I thought perhaps a hundred at the most might respond, but more than seven hundred people got in the prayer line. For at least two hours, the prophet of the Lord and I cast out demons — and not just one demon out of each person. Some of those people had several in them. They were born again and filled with the Holy Spirit, but they did not understand why they were not happy. The devil had stolen their joy from them.

Later, we discovered that we had created quite a ruckus in the spirit world by setting those people free. After the service we went to a restaurant because when you have cast out thousands of demons, you are tired and hungry. You have literally been through warfare.

We sat in a private room shielded from the other rooms in the restaurant by blinds. We had been there for about twenty minutes, talking about what God had done, when two young women walked in who had not been in the meeting. They sat down in the next room, peeked at us through the blinds, and the demons in them began to shout, "There they are!" At first, it did not dawn on me what they were talking about. Then they began to holler and make fun of us. They screamed, "Those are the ones who hurt us tonight. Those are the ones we need to be careful of. We need to be careful of them because they are powerful."

When you become an invading force, things like that will begin to happen to you, and you will know you are a big threat to the kingdom of darkness. Don't be afraid! It is time to rejoice when demons get upset and scream at you.

That experience proved to me that I was on the right track. When you start invading, you will become known in the natural world as well as in the spiritual. There will be battles against your family, your church, your job, and every aspect of your life. But remember — the Greater One lives inside you.

Ye are of God, little children, and have overcome them: because greater is he that is in you, than he that is in the world.

1 John 4:4

You have power over all the works of the devil. You are mighty on this earth because God has given you His power to perform His works on this earth. My friends, our generation is the generation that Joel and Peter prophesied about. We are that invading force. This revival is not like all the others. The truths of all the others will be in this revival, but this is a new one. All the revivals of the past were defensive, but this one is an all-out attack. We are going to be an invading force!

Chapter 3

Unending Revival

What is *revival?* A revival is experiencing an intense presence of God on the earth. Revival is literally feeling the presence of God walking up and down the aisles of churches. A revival is when men come into contact with an invisible being, and they cannot deny that there is a real, unseen force called God in their midst.

In the early days of creation, Adam walked in the Spirit of God and set the trend for all subsequent moves of God's Spirit. The Lord once told me, "I have always started the moves, but men always stopped them. I never designed for revival to end. I started it on the day of creation. I meant for it to last forever on the planet called earth. But because of the fall of man revival stopped, and it is difficult for them to get back in the flow of it again."

Those who live in the realm of the spirit live in constant revival because the spirit realm is constantly moving — a constant revival. When men turn their hearts back to

God in a new obedience and a new commitment, revival will begin to spread across the earth. When men get desperate, crying out for God and living in the realm of the spirit, revival will break out.

God never designed for revival to end. He meant for revival to continue forever. Revival stops when Christians get lazy. But in the days to come, the revivals of the past and the truths brought forth in those moves will combine with a new blast of God's glory. It will be the greatest outpouring of the Holy Spirit the world has ever seen or felt. The gates of hell cannot prevail against this move that is coming to the earth. No religious organization will organize it out of existence. No one will preach it to death. It is coming, and it is coming full force.

Revival Now

People in heaven are very much aware of the happenings on earth. They are very much aware of what you are doing for the kingdom of God. They even pray for the saints who are on the earth. Ephesians 1:10 states that we are one family in heaven and in earth. We are not two separate families — we are one. What the family in heaven has, we on earth can have. That same presence, that same peace, and that same power belong to us on earth. We do not have to wait to go to heaven to enjoy God's presence or power. They belong to us now.

Many people do not want to pay the price for God's glory. They want to ride on the coattails of other people, but coattails are becoming short. No one can piggyback you into God's glory.

I believe some will call this coming revival a selfish revival because it is going to be only for those who will seek it. This revival is not going to come to men like past revivals did. In God's sovereign moves of the past, He always met men, but I believe this new move has come as far as it is going to come. Now we must go out to meet it if we are to be part of it. That is the difference between this outpouring and all the outpourings of the past.

That is what is causing the great separation we presently see among the people of God. Many are puzzled because there is no confusion or strife in this new move. They do not understand that when you get in the flow of revival, there cannot be confusion or strife. Slowly but surely, this age is coming to an end. God's moves in this age are getting less frequent. Because of this, we must go to where the move of God is. We must go into the world of the spirit.

Sermons that Change People's Lives

I do not understand it when preachers say they can only preach fifteen minutes. Believe me, if you are called you can preach at least an hour. If you have done your homework you can preach at least two hours. When I lecture in Bible schools,

I have fifty-five minutes to deliver my two-hour sermon. The students just look at me because they cannot take notes fast enough. They say, "How can you talk that fast?" I reply, "It does not come through my head. It comes out of my heart." That is the big difference.

Sermons that will change people's lives are not educational "one, two, three" sermons. They are heartfelt, Holy Spirit sermons — sermons born out of hours of intercession for the people to whom we are to minister. Success does not come to those who have perfect words, movements, and pulpit etiquette. Success comes to those who have gotten hold of God Almighty. When men and women like that walk out on the platform and say, "Hello," the power of God falls. That is what the earth needs today. The people of the world and people in dying churches are not looking for an unlimited move of the Holy Spirit. But we must take it to them anyway.

Heaven places no limits or boundaries on the moving of the Holy Spirit. The presence of God flows and does anything it wants to in heaven. There should never be limits or boundaries on the flow of God's Spirit in your church or in your life. Keep yourself open to the unction of the Holy Spirit. Let God know you are one He can use to fulfill His purpose on this earth.

God Is Not Weird

The flow of the Spirit of God should not be weird. God is not weird, and He does not like it when believers claim that their weirdness is "walking in the Spirit." I am 100 percent against people who say they are in the Spirit when they actually are in the flesh. They are weird! They will not listen to someone who acts normal — someone who is in the Spirit.

Just because I do not roll down the aisle with them, they think I am not in the Spirit. Well, I do not roll down aisles, but God can knock me down aisles. I am not against the movings of the Holy Spirit. I am not against the unusual. I am not even against the strange, but I am totally against the weird. God does not bless weirdness and He does not bless flakiness.

There will be a great deal of weirdness in the new glory move, if people who are real do not stand up when someone does something out of the flesh — or influenced by a demon — and declare, "That is not of God. Change!" There must be an authority and a standard established in this new move of God, and if something does not meet that standard it should not be received as having come from God. All the past moves of God failed because of people who got weird, people who went to extremes, and others who went off and did what they wanted rather than what God wanted.

The Secret of the Next Move

Do not tell God what to do — He tells you what to do. Do not try to manufacture the gifts or moving of the precious

Holy Spirit. It cannot be done. In this new move we are coming into, we have to be so careful that we do not grieve the Holy Spirit because He is the secret of this next move of God. We have to become His very, very best friend. We have to know how to walk and talk with Him. We cannot afford to make one wrong move or speak one wrong word when the Holy Spirit is moving.

If you have a message in tongues or an interpretation, make sure it comes from the heart of God and not from your own heart. That is one of the things that causes the Holy Spirit to lift, and He might be gone for two months. Some people just do not know any better, and I realize that. However, there are those who do know better, but who stand up and give a nice word that is not for the entire congregation, but for their own hearts. When someone gets out of line like that, it grieves the Holy Spirit. We are moving into a very intense place — a realm of the Spirit where we have to be obedient. We have to know the Holy Spirit, be sensitive to His voice and His direction, and be quick to obey.

Flesh or Spirit?

We have to learn to listen to the Holy Spirit's wooings and teachings so we will not take the wrong path or do the wrong things. We are standing at a crossroads in our relationship with God. No longer will He bless those who operate in the flesh. No longer will He bless those who call the flesh "spirituality." He will withdraw His presence and go where people are truly hungry, truly willing to learn, and truly willing to flow with the Holy Spirit. He will go where there are no personalities trying to be popular.

God is the only one who should ever get any glory. It is not men who bring the moves of God. It is not even men who carry the moves. It is the Holy Spirit who brings revival and keeps it going as long as people keep yielding and humbling themselves and saying, "God, whatever…do it."

There is a stirring within me. I have studied church history and the moves of John Wesley, Martin Luther, the Voice of Healing organization, and many others, and I have seen how many preachers fell. Then I look at this move we are entering, knowing it will be the greatest move the earth will ever see, and I cannot keep quiet. I cannot allow people to do what they want to in the flesh, claiming they are doing it in the name of God. If it is not of God, they must be corrected. They must be told to keep quiet and sit down for the sake of the outpouring of the Holy Spirit.

We must have a standard. Pastors and evangelists must have the manhood and womanhood to stand up for God, to stand up for what is right, and to come against what is wrong. Pastor, do not allow your church to go off the deep end. Do not allow your people to rule you. God has placed you over them. You are the one who is the head of that congregation, so you instruct your sheep. Explain to them what is the moving of God, and what is of the flesh. Show them and teach them how to discern the difference for themselves because you can't be with them every moment of every day.

We have to understand how the Holy Spirit moves. The way He moves throughout heaven must become the way He moves throughout the earth. In the prayer services in heaven, no one tries to become the leader or director. They gather together in the unity of faith and the Spirit, joined together in the divine love that is in their hearts. They look toward the throne room of God, and as the songs within them begin to swell, no one tries to outsing the others. No one is saying, "I danced better than you." They are flowing together to make one voice and one sound that is heard throughout all of heaven, making the heart of God jump for joy.

We must get to that unity of the Spirit for this outpouring of the Holy Spirit to flow as it is supposed to and for the miracles to happen as they are supposed to. We must have that standard in line with the Holy Spirit. We cannot do what we want to do. We are not to promote our own selves or our own ministry, but we must promote the Lord Jesus Christ. Let Him be the popular Person. Let Him be the personality. Let Him receive the glory, honor, praise, and worship that are due Him.

The Importance of Being Yielded

As I look at people in a congregation, I see those who have flowed with the mighty hand of God, and I see others who have flowed only partially. We must operate totally in the flow of the Holy Spirit and learn to yield ourselves to Him. He is the very secret of the power of the Trinity. He is the one who causes people to be healed. It is His power that does it. No one else is the Healer. People who have miracles in their services are yielded to Him. They know better than anyone else that they do not have the power to heal. It is God who heals as the Holy Spirit flows through them.

We need to become doors without locks and windows that are always open — always available to Him. We have to be able to say to the Holy Spirit, "Here I am. Flow through me. Do what You want. I will go. I will speak. I will be quiet. I will be still. Whatever You desire, Holy Spirit, I will do for the promotion of the kingdom of God."

We do not have to touch people to get them healed. We do not even have to direct a prayer to a specific person for them to be healed. If we learn to let the Holy Spirit speak and flow through our very being, He will heal people as we proclaim the Good News.

Not by might, nor by power, but by my spirit, saith the Lord of hosts.

Zechariah 4:6

We stand at a place where we must humble ourselves. Sadly, many people are seeking personal popularity. They think that if they can get on the platform or if they can give a message in tongues and get recognized, God will use them more. However, if you are seeking your own popularity or promotion, God cannot use you.

Just say, "God, I am yielded. Whatever You want is fine with me." If He decides to use you at this particular point, fine. If not, fine. But know this, if you are truly seeking Him in all your ways, He will use you.

When I first started in the ministry, people were always asking me, "What is your secret? How do you go out on the stage and preach those wild sermons? What is the secret of walking into a congregation and having half the congregation falling under the power when you say, 'Hello'? What is the secret?"

The secret is that God is looking for holy, yielded vessels to use. That is why it is necessary for us to have a *relationship* with Jesus. We must *know* Him. When we are in relationship with Jesus, we make ourselves available to the Holy Spirit. We are yielded to the Holy Spirit. We will be obedient to the Holy Spirit.

Nevertheless I tell you the truth; It is expedient for you that I go away: for if I go not away, the Comforter will not come unto you; but if I depart, I will send him unto you.

And when he is come, he will reprove the world of sin, and of righteousness, and of judgment;

Of sin, because they believe not on me;

Of righteousness, because I go to my Father, and ye see me no more;

Of judgment, because the prince of this world is judged.

I have yet many things to say unto you, but ye cannot bear them now.

Howbeit when he, the Spirit of truth, is come, he will guide you into all truth: for he shall not speak of himself; but whatsoever he shall hear, that shall he speak: and he will shew you things to come.

He shall glorify me: for he shall receive of mine, and shall shew it unto you.

John 16:7-14

The Holy Spirit is our Teacher. People want the Holy Spirit to flow in their lives and ministries, but often they try to accomplish that by their own achievements. God is not impressed by our achievements! Yieldedness and humility attract God to a person, then He moves through them.

You do not delight in sacrifice, or I would bring it; you do not take pleasure in burnt offerings.

The sacrifices of God are a broken spirit; a broken and contrite heart, O God, you will not despise.

Psalm 51:16-17 NIV

Smith Wigglesworth was an uneducated plumber whose wife had to teach him how to read. He stammered, stuttered, and could not speak proper English, but when the Holy Spirit fell on him, Smith Wigglesworth would yield to the Spirit and speak as well as any English professor.

We yield to the Holy Spirit by obeying Him. It isn't a magnetic personality or a great organization that brings revival, it is the Holy Spirit flowing through yielded vessels. Organizations may come out of revival and personalities may spring forth, but the key is always the Holy Spirit flowing through yielded individuals.

The Importance of Being Humble

Never build your life or ministry on an *experience*. You can share your experience and help many people, but that experience will not carry you through the storms of life. What will carry you through the storms of life is understanding and cooperating with the Trinity and the Word of God.

Never deviate from the Word of God. Never get so spiritual that you try to outdo the Bible. Never get so high and mighty that you think you know more than Matthew, Mark, Luke, and John. You will never reach a place that you do not need to listen to the Holy Spirit. You must never tell the Holy Spirit what to do. You must wait for Him to tell you what to do.

The Holy Spirit is to be to us today what Jesus was to His disciples. Jesus taught them, "This is the way you should go." When they deviated from that way, He said, "Stop! Woe be unto you. Satan, get off them!"

The Holy Spirit corrects us the same way. The first thing He does is speak to our heart to impress upon us, "This is not right. Don't do that. That is not of Me." He does overlook ignorance because His love is so great and His mercy endures forever. He will plead with us, "Please, please, don't do it. Please, go this way. Don't go that way." We must learn to listen to the wooings and impressions from the Holy Spirit because we cannot continue to do whatever we want to do and keep the presence of the Holy Spirit in our lives.

In the past, certain preachers have acted as if they were superstars of the religious world. Two noted preachers have actually claimed to be Elijah. As soon as they did this they began to fall, and their falls were very hard.

We do not need any more failures in the ministry, especially in this move into which we are entering. When someone falls, it is a mark against the Church. It hinders the world from seeing Jesus. It is like a knife slashing the very heart of God because once you yield yourself to God, He takes out a guarantee on your life. He says, "Heaven, we can trust this person. He is committed."

Then God starts pouring out the power. He starts pouring out the glory. He starts opening doors of utterance to you, putting you before great and mighty men, and giving you influence and divine favor. As long as you use the influence to promote the kingdom of God and the moving of the Holy Spirit on the earth, your anointing, your promotions, and the outpouring of the Holy Spirit in your services will increase.

If you start saying, "Look at me. Look at what I can do," you might become like Samson. He woke up one morning without any power because he had been fooling around with the wrong world. When his enemies came to get him, Samson shook himself and tried to use his supernatural strength, but there was no strength and his enemies overtook him. (See Judges 16:19-21.)

I have seen many ministers grace the pulpit, and as they began to speak they shook themselves, but there was nothing. They said, "Hello," and there was no power. They went back to their nice little three-point sermons that were dried up and dead, and their ministries dwindled away. Some who lost their anointing backslid against God and died. They got mad at God and screamed, "Why have You forsaken me?" They did not have enough sense to understand that they had forsaken Him when they deviated from the way they should have gone. They took the power and began using it for self-gain. You can do that for only so long until the judgment of God will come. That judgment will be equal to your anointing — the stronger the anointing, the stronger the judgment.

Brother So-and-So's power was known throughout the earth. It used to be that when he came to town, if you could get to his services, God would meet you there. He would speak to you. He would heal the sick and save the lost.

People would come by the thousands and fill the auditoriums. Brother So-and-So would come to the podium, open the service as usual, and the excitement would rage high. As he began to preach, however, the excitement began to decrease. People wondered, "What is the matter with Brother So-and-So? Well, he must be tired. He has been on the mission field, and he is so exhausted."

He comes to town again the next year, and the same thing happens. People say, "Well, what is wrong now? Maybe he is under persecution." But when you are under persecution, that is the time you should glory the most. That is when the glory should be the greatest. That is when God says, "He is My servant. Watch what I do in behalf of his words!" And the people wonder at what God does.

Knowing the Holy Spirit

You must not grieve the Holy Spirit. You must not move out from the shadow of the Almighty. Do not simply *visit* the world of the spirit. Go there to abide in the shadow of the Almighty. Learn to live in the presence of the Trinity. Learn to walk and to talk with them. Let the things of this world drop off. Let your eyes no longer look downward, but let them look upward into the presence of the Most High. Let your desires be on the things that are above and not on the things that are beneath.

Know that no tape or book will ever promote a ministry the way God intends. No popular man who takes you under his wing and promotes your ministry will cause you to succeed. The only thing that will cause any ministry or lay person to succeed in what they are called to do is being yielded in prayer and in speaking to the people of the Lord. It is not *men's* words that God wants you to speak. It is *His* words the people need to hear, and God wants to speak through you.

The only way you will get those words is by learning to yield yourself to the Holy Spirit. Those who work with you also must learn to flow in the unity of the Spirit. Where there is strife, there is no order or move of the Holy Spirit. One wrong song can cause the power of God to lift. One wrong action can cause the glory of God to lift. However, one right action can cause the power to fall. That is why you must know the desire of the Holy Spirit for that service.

We need to *know* the Holy Spirit. Learning *about* Him isn't enough. We need to know Him the way He really is. What does He like? What does He dislike? What causes His power to increase in a service? What causes it to decrease? Having an intimate relationship with Jesus and walking in the spirit rather than the flesh will bring God's power to our lives and to our ministries. We will see miracles in our services. The Holy Spirit will convict people's hearts and those who don't know Jesus will get saved. When you know the Holy Spirit and rely on Him, God's power will fall and minister effectively to His people.

Supernatural Feats

We are moving into a place that if the Church does not produce what she has been talking about, she is going to be sawn asunder. No, I am not preaching doom and gloom. I am saying, "Wake up, look, and move!"

What is the Church going to do when rock stars and spiritualists come out on stage and say, "We are the answer for the world," and perform supernatural feats before the cameras? Are we going to do as the Church did in the past — ignore it and say, "It will go away"? We have said that long enough, and it has not passed away. The only way that kind of deception is going to be destroyed is when a man or a woman of God comes out on the other side of that stage and proclaims, "Our God is greater. Watch this — POW."

For too long, the Church has allowed the world to plunge deeper and deeper into sin. For too long, the preachers have spoken empty words, "We will preach the Gospel. We will walk in love." The love of God stands up for what is right and proclaims the truth. It is time we get back to that. It is time we get the Holy Ghost and fire in our bones so we can rise up against evil things — not in wondering, not in doubt and unbelief, but in sure confidence that God will show Himself strong.

What are you going to do, Church, when your children and your young people see those rock stars and spiritualists perform definite miracles by evil power on television? Some believe the devil has no power. That is not the truth! I have seen the devil do too many things. I have heard too many true stories and have seen what the power of darkness can do in other countries. Most Americans do not know what goes on in foreign nations. They have not yet experienced the confrontation with evil that Africans and Europeans have seen.

The Holy Spirit has spoken to me and to other men of God that America is under the greatest attack of the enemy she has ever seen, and it is only going to grow stronger and stronger. A standard must be raised up. A people of power must come forth who will say, "Our God is still Almighty."

Several years ago, a preacher with a little group behind him, egging him on, brought in newspapermen as he prayed for people who had been given up to die. His plan fell through. The sick people did not get healed. What a mockery against the Church! It hurt my heart. I know this kind of thing continues to happen, but we do not need disaster cases.

I went to prayer and said, "God, I know Your Word is true. Why did this man fail?"

The Lord spoke to me and said, "Those people were trying to build a reputation for their church and their ministry. They were trying to make themselves known."

When you take on warfare like that, you have to make sure that you died to self a long time ago. You have to make sure you are not in charge because you are powerless without the Holy Spirit flowing through you. Remember, you do not tell Him what to do, He tells you what to do.

Confrontations Are Coming

I saw a vision when I was preaching at a convention in Tulsa, Oklahoma, in 1984. I saw a stage and the television networks taping a confrontation of evil and good. I saw the people of the devil and their leaders on one side of the stage, and the people of God and their leaders on the other side.

The devil's side began to perform miracles and supernatural feats. They would strike someone blind, and the people of God would get them healed. The devil's side would cause someone to be crippled, and one from God's side would say, "Be healed," and the people were healed, one right after the other.

When God vindicates Himself, He does it in a profitable manner. He does not destroy people. He does not kill the flesh. The devil is the one who kills. When God begins to move like this, know that He will not destroy His creation to prove His point. Instead, He will bless it. He will cause it to be greater because God is a God of greatness and of love.

We are at a place where the people of God must stand up and confront evil forces. The earth is getting increasingly evil and the kingdom of darkness is getting worse. We must learn how to get in the realm of the spirit and flow with Him so we will not be left powerless and in doubt and unbelief. Instead, we will be full of confidence and faith. We will say, "Come on, you prophets of Baal. We will show you who has the fire. We will show you whose God reigns."

Those confrontations are coming. When they begin to occur, respect for the Church will return. Men who now slur God's name will go off our television screens. People in the media will have respect when they see a person of God. Their whole mentality and the way in which they speak to us will change. One reason the world laughs at the Church today and laughs at you for being a Christian is because we seem so powerless. We have all the knowledge in the world about chapter and verse, but we need to combine that knowledge with old-fashioned, Pentecostal fire in order to go forth in God's power.

When someone doubts God, prove God to him! Let God be real. Let God be manifested in our presence. Let us so walk with the presence of God that miracles happen everywhere we go. Let those who speak against us have their mouths stopped as they watch in amazement the things God does on our behalf. If you will yield yourself to the Holy Spirit, God will turn heaven and earth upside down to answer your cry and your prayer.

God's arm is not shortened that He cannot save, and His ear is not deaf that He cannot hear you. Get under the shadow of the Almighty, and go forth proclaiming the Good News with signs following.

Preparing for the Future

People have the attitude that the Word will do the work all by itself. The Word is mighty and powerful, but the Word cannot work in the fullness it is supposed to unless the vessel proclaiming it is up to par with God's standard. The vessel must be full of the Holy Spirit and power, know the secret of the power of the Holy Spirit (being yielded), and be dead to self. Unless these qualifications are met, a man or a woman cannot go forth and raise the dead and cause the lost to come to the Lord.

We stand at a crossroads today. We have a decision to make. The things we go through are preparing us and teaching us for what is going to come in the future. The kingdom of darkness is going to be great in the earth, but the kingdom of light must be greater and more powerful, and we must know what we are doing.

No longer can we play games with God. No longer can we make fun of God and His chosen vessels. No longer can we be in strife. No longer can we dislike our brother or sister. We must walk in love, and we must know what we are doing when the devil confronts us saying, "Where is your God?" We have to be able to say, "Here He is" — BAM! And the devil is off and running with his tail between his legs!

We can have all the nice testimonies in the world, but in this day and time, the testimonies may not need to be spoken. Instead, that old-time Holy Ghost fire needs to be delivered from the mouths of God's prophets into the midst of His people. There needs to come a stirring in the hearts of people that will cause them to go into their prayer rooms, fall on their faces, and call on God to fill their lives with the power to do what He wants them to do.

Powerless Christians are not worth talking to. Their witness is dead. I have looked at some who go out on witnessing teams, these soul-winning adventures. Yes, they are adventures for the soul-winners because they never get anyone saved! But if you are equipped with God's power, you will see multitudes come to the Lord.

You do not have to be eloquent, you just have to have the power to produce. You say, "That's heavy." Well, it is heavy out there. No longer is it "nice" in the world. In the early days of this country, God's people were respected. But in the 1920s, the Church began to go off into its own world. Christians said, "We will just leave the world to itself. We want to have our bless-me-clubs — just us four, just rolling around in the Lord." What has happened since the Church has been rolling? The world has taken over!

The Overcoming Life

God is speaking the same message to different bands of believers. Coming from different parts of the country and not knowing each other, they are arriving in cities saying, "Take this city for My glory." We are seeing this happen not just in America, but throughout the world. These believers are invading the devil's territory and winning!

Let the earth fear the Church of the Lord Jesus Christ. Let the demons fear the faces of the Christians today. Let the kingdom of darkness know your name as Christ's name is known. Let the kingdom of darkness know you are not afraid to fight. We are the victors. (See 1 John 5:4.) We are more than conquerors. (See Romans 8:37.) We are the overcomers in the earth today. (See 1 John 2:13.)

Those who persecute us and speak out against the outpouring of the Holy Spirit and against those flowing in the power of God will come to naught before too long. They will know God is in His people. They will know God is moving in a new way — a way unlike anything you have ever heard or seen before. God's angels will walk hand in hand with the believers, taking on the powers of darkness in combat. We are going to battle, we are going to fight, and we are going to win.

People tell me, "You should not talk about the devil." But look what happened because you did not talk about him — he almost killed you! You do not have to glorify the devil. Just recognize that he is the problem and attack. If you ignore the devil, he will get you every time. You have to say, "There is the enemy — there is the source of my problem. Come on, let's destroy the source." Take your confessions and prayers, put them right in the face of the devil, and drive him out of the way.

Let that holy anger rise up within you — a righteous indignation. You have to get ruthless in this warfare. The

Bible says, **the kingdom of heaven suffereth violence, and the violent take it by force** (Matthew 11:12). You be the violent! You get rough. You get tough. You get into this battle with everything you have, and I guarantee you'll be victorious. God is on your side!

Knowing Your Enemy

We have brothers and sisters who are are talking this and talking that, confessing this and dancing to that, and saying, "God is good. Hallelujah!" But the entire time, right next to them a demon-possessed person may be doing the same thing. Then they wonder why a certain church with forty people is experiencing a massive move of God, and nothing is happening in their church of four hundred. God doesn't look at numbers like man does. I would rather have a small church of on-fire believers than a huge church with lukewarm believers.

We have to drive out the powers of darkness. The Lord told me not too long ago, "Americans make up the greatest nation on the earth today, but they also have one great problem — they are being possessed and oppressed faster than the people of any other nation."

If a demon is occupying the mind or body of a Christian, it will cramp the Holy Spirit to where He cannot move. When people are bound, they cannot raise their hands or dance before the Lord in their churches. They do not know what is wrong, so they say, "We've got it all together." That is what they think. But really they have it all "un-together." If they cannot dance up and down the aisles of the churches here, they are bound up by something.

If you do not believe in fighting devils, what are you going to do when a horde of them comes knocking at your door? Invite them in for supper?

"I just won't answer the door."

Well, they just might come in through the window! We should not be ignorant of the devil's devices. We do not need to be frightened, but we do need to know who our enemy is. How can a military force fight an enemy which it knows nothing about? How can they be prepared? When a war is going on, spies are sent in to study the enemy and see what he is doing. We in the body of Christ need to send our spies in also. There are spiritual spies in the earth today. They are called prophets, and they are coming to you with God's message: "Arise Church, and put on your armor. Don't let the sun go down on your wrath. Do not be in strife with one another, but join yourselves in faith and in unity and seek My face. Go forth."

God spoke to me about an army. What is an army for? Are we just going to dress in armor for the sake of wearing armor?

God always has a purpose in everything He does. He never does anything just for the sake of doing it.

An army does not tiptoe around its enemy — it attacks its enemy. As the army of God, we need to be equipped with the proper battle attire. We need to be dressed in the full armor of God.

> Finally, my brethren, be strong in the Lord, and in the power of his might.
>
> Put on the whole armour of God, that ye may be able to stand against the wiles of the devil.
>
> For we wrestle not against flesh and blood, but against principalities, against powers, against the rulers of the darkness of this world, against spiritual wickedness in high places.
>
> Wherefore take unto you the whole armour of God, that ye may be able to withstand in the evil day, and having done all, to stand.
>
> Stand therefore, having your loins girt about with truth, and having on the breastplate of righteousness;
>
> And your feet shod with the preparation of the gospel of peace;
>
> Above all, taking the shield of faith, wherewith ye shall be able to quench all the fiery darts of the wicked.
>
> And take the helmet of salvation, and the sword of the Spirit, which is the Word of God.
>
> Praying always with all prayer and supplication in the Spirit.
>
> **Ephesians 6:10-18**

It is time we start knocking the enemy back and possessing the land that belongs to the kingdom of God. It is time we took back what the devil has stolen. It is time we took back the earth. The earth and the fullness thereof belong to the Lord and His joint-heirs. The prosperity of this world belongs to the Church. The land belongs to us. There is no need for anyone to lack or be in despair because God has given it to us. We must rise up in the power of His might, take our armor, go forth into battle, and reclaim what belongs to the Church.

Jesus Paid for Prosperity

Beloved, I wish above all things that thou mayest prosper and be in health, even as thy soul prospereth.
3 John 2

Do you know why some believers do not have any money? They have not gotten violent enough to get it. They gripe about some preacher asking them to give money in the offering, but if they would give as the Lord directs, the preachers wouldn't have to ask. If people understood what the Word has to say about finances, ministers wouldn't have to beg and plead with congregations to get offerings large enough just to meet expenses. More than enough would come in!

Dominion over the entire planet originally belonged to mankind, but we sinned and gave that dominion to the enemy. Then Christ came and took back all the power and the keys from Satan and said to us, "Go ye into all the world and preach the Gospel. Proclaim unto them that this world is the Lord's, and if they want to be in the kingdom that is going to rule, they need to get on God's side."

It is going to take money to get this earth back. People do not like to hear that because money is the one thing they have not died to. You do not own your money. In fact, what is a green bill compared to golden streets? Do not gripe about someone who got violent enough to get out of poverty and into prosperity. You should say, "How did you do it? Teach me."

I am also totally against sickness and poverty because I believe with all my heart that Jesus Christ has paid in full for our healing and prosperity. (See Isaiah 53:5.) We have the right and the authority in Christ Jesus to reclaim that which was stolen from us and possess what belongs to us. Get mad at the devil for stealing your finances, your health, and your family! Get mad enough to do something about it. Tell the devil, "Devil, watch out! Here I come to get everything back that you stole from me. No longer am I going to sit back and feel sorry for myself. Today, things are going to change!"

Financing the Gospel

After the United States won World War II, its representatives went into the conquered countries and gave them money to rebuild and get back on their feet. That is what the Church must do, and the dollars, shillings, and pounds must come to the Church. That is one reason God tells us to be prosperous.

God is moving all over the world. We in North America need to start pouring all the extra money we have, after we have paid our bills and have our needs met, into world evangelism. We need to start pouring it into organizations and ministries, or even take a vacation to go someplace and preach.

God sent me to Uganda to preach when I was nineteen years old. After flying for over twenty hours, I arrived and went straight to the auditorium to address the people. I did not have time to comb my hair or change my clothes. I felt so dirty, but those people were so hungry that they did not mind. They were not concerned about my rumpled clothes or that I was only nineteen years old. They did not ask if I was a pastor, if I had a big ministry, or if I was a popular minister. They were only concerned that I had the Word of God to give them. They were just glad I was there. The only thing they asked was, "Teach us about Jesus. Teach us about the Holy Spirit. Teach us about the Gospel, please." That is all they were looking for.

There are lost and dying people in every nation who desperately need to hear the Gospel message. The world is not going to finance the Gospel — Christians must finance the Gospel. Our desire should be to have more money, but our motivation should be to give more into missions and world evangelism. You may not be able to travel to other countries as a missionary, but as you give to missions, you become a part of that work. People will accept Jesus because you gave of your finances.

Reclaiming the Territory

Invading the devil's territory involves a reclaiming of that territory. What God meant for us the devil has stolen, and it is time to reclaim it! We need to get back to the violence of the Gospel. I did not say to get *brutal*. I said to get violent. We need to come in with our sword, our shield, and our feet shod, glowing from head to foot, saying, "Devil, move over. You are going to get it!"

If he does not move over when you tell him to, jab him with chapter and verse. The day will come when the devil will say, "When (put your own name here) comes, it's time for us to leave!" Wouldn't you just love to kick Satan off this planet? If the Church of the Lord Jesus Christ would stand up to the devil and take back what belongs to us, we would tie the devil up so that he could not move.

The devil is not going to give anything back without a fight. No enemy is going to let you take them over without opposition. That is why governments have to send troops in to clear out the territory after a battle. We are going to have to clear out the territory, possess it, and rebuild it.

When Jesus comes for the Church, He will be looking for an active Church, a Church that says, "Yes, we are working. We are doing what you commissioned us to do." He will be looking for a Church that is glorious, without spot or wrinkle. And one way to get out spots and wrinkles is to *work* them out.

The day will come when the people of God will rise up and be so powerful that they will invade cities and nations; and when they leave that city or nation, the powers of the devil will have been so broken that his presence will not even be seen or felt there anymore. That shall come to pass. It is coming! It looks impossible, but my God specializes in impossibilities.

With men it is impossible, but not with God: for with God all things are possible.

Mark 10:27

Putting Action to the Vision

God never gives a vision to any man or woman which they can achieve in their own human strength. He always gives them something to do that takes every ounce of faith just to believe He has called them to do it. That is a vision. To accomplish the vision, however, they have to be obedient, and they have to walk in faith.

That is where we stand today. The pew needs some action and the pulpit needs some violence. If the pulpit gets some violence, so will the pew. We need to get off our pews, go out into this dying world, and let people know there is a God! Let them know He is not dead, that our God is alive. If they do not believe it, pray in tongues and shout, let God do a few miracles, and they will get saved. They will believe it.

I believe the day is coming when miracles will become almost commonplace where you are. If people say, "No, there is no God," in your presence, you will pray miracles into manifestation. It is coming. I do not care what unbelief or doubt may tell you, nothing can stop this great outpouring of the Holy Spirit.

Whether you like it or not, the day you got saved was the day you were recruited to be in God's army. But the good news is that you are part of an army that is guaranteed victory every time! That's the army to be in — an army that causes the enemy to shake with fear.

How has God called you to be an invading force? If you are not sure, take time today to ask Him. Be *determined* to be a powerful force. Be *determined* to stomp all over the enemy and bring about the destruction of his evil ways. Be *determined* to obey God in what He calls you to do. Don't worry about not having enough knowledge because God will equip you for whatever comes your way.

There may be times that seem like you are fighting a losing battle, but as I said earlier in the book, do not grow weary in well doing. (See Galatians 6:9.) You can invade the devil's territory and take back all he has stolen from you. And not only can you take back what belongs to you, Proverbs 6:31 tells us the thief must restore it to us sevenfold. Be aggressive in defeating the enemy and reclaiming the territory. Don't be afraid to move into the realm of the Holy Spirit. Go on into those new worlds. Be part of God's invading force!

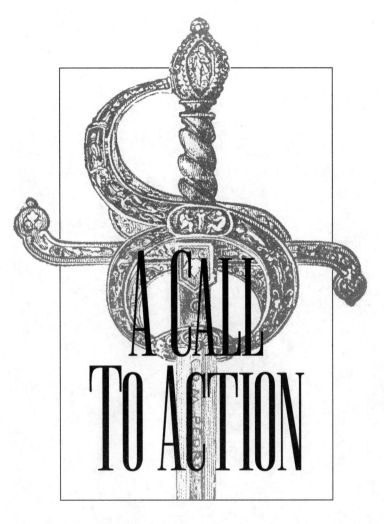

A CALL TO ACTION

Killing Giants and Subduing Kingdoms

ROBERTS LIARDON

DEDICATION

I dedicate this book to the memory of my Grandpa LeBasker Moore who set the trend for my family to preach and live for God. Grandpa ministered the saving and healing power of Jesus Christ in the churches of the North Carolina area. He was anointed of God as an evangelist and singer. "His singing drew the crowds," Grandma says, "while the Holy Spirit sparked revival, bringing salvation and healing to many."

Grandpa, saved and filled with the Holy Spirit at a very young age, began preaching when he was 12 years old. His parents were Christians, and his own father possessed an unquenchable compassion for people. The winds of the Spirit blew through Grandpa's meetings, and multitudes were literally slain in the Spirit without a hand touching them. Although Grandpa lacked knowledge of the Word of God compared with today's standards, his meetings never lacked the power of God.

Grandma says of Grandpa, "He was a man who lived what he preached. He did not preach one thing and live something else. He had such a beautiful relationship with the Lord that he would often say, 'God just poured a tub of honey on my soul.'"

Although I do not remember my Grandpa personally, since he passed away when I was a small child, Grandma believes the anointing of God upon his life was imparted to me as he held me and rocked me as a baby.

Grandpa was born October 12, 1896, and went on to his eternal home on September 16, 1967. He left his mark upon my life, for which I am grateful to God. It encourages me tremendously to know that Grandpa daily cheers me on in the things of God from heaven's grandstands! (See Hebrews 12:1.)

Grandma says he had many favorite scriptures, but two that stand out are **Let not the sun go down upon your wrath** (Ephesians 4:26) and **O taste and see that the Lord is good** (Psalm 34:8).

Contents

FOREWORD

I first met Roberts Liardon when he was fifteen years old. After my first lengthy conversation with him, I was amazed at the young man's spiritual maturity and fascinated by his depth and breadth of knowledge regarding the great spiritual leaders of the Church, especially those of the Divine Healing/Pentecostal/ Charismatic movements. As a church historian with five earned degrees, I was absolutely astounded with the ease and fluidity with which Roberts could dialogue with me regarding these giants of the faith. Few scholars have the knowledge and insights that Roberts possesses regarding the great leaders of the Divine Healing/Pentecostal/Charismatic movements. I vividly remember going out of my way the day following our first conversation to ask his mother what it was like to have a 15 year old with the maturity of a 35 year old residing in her household!

Since that initial conversation, Roberts and I have had many delightful times sharing about the giants of the faith. I have even had him lecture to my graduate seminary classes — he may be the first teenager to lecture to a graduate theology class in the twentieth century. He was always an inspiration to our graduate students. Roberts also lectured regularly at one of the Bible colleges here in Tulsa.

Roberts is a very special young man. His knowledge, his maturity, and his experience are far beyond his years. God has called this young man into His holy service, and Roberts has diligently been obedient to that divine call. What other teenager do you know who has traveled extensively across the United States, Europe, and Africa carrying the message of Christ and praying effectively for the healing of the sick? On one such trip Roberts made an extensive, two-month evangelistic trip to Africa, where he preached not only in large cities, but also spent much of his time in the bush country ministering to the tribal people. Roberts has truly taken God's Word to where God's voice is heard small and where His light is seen dimly.

When I was a young child, my father taught me that I could gain experience and maturity far beyond my years if I would but learn from the experiences of those older than myself. Over the years I've learned that his advice was solid. When Roberts was 11 years old, his heavenly Father told him to "study the lives of the generals in My great army. Know why they succeeded and why they failed." Since then, Roberts has immersed himself in studying many of the great spiritual leaders of the Church.

You see, the past is more than a fossil. It is a teacher and an illuminator of God's truth and will. When one immerses himself in the study of the spiritual giants of the past, he soon feels dwarfed and humbled in their presence. A spirit of humility and teachableness results from such a study. A study of how God has worked in the lives of the great spiritual leaders of the past also provides present-day believers with guidance and direction for their own lives. C. S. Lewis's *Screwtape Letters* encourages us to study the lives of the great saints when it records the senior devil giving the following advice to a junior devil:

Since we cannot deceive the whole human race all the time, it is most important to cut every generation off from all others; for where learning makes a free commerce between the ages there is always the danger that the characteristic errors of one may be corrected by the characteristic truth of another.

The serious Christian of the present needs to always be interested in studying and learning from the successes and failures of the spiritual giants of the Church. Church history teaches us that believers continually need God's forgiveness, instruction, and guidance. God can instruct us through the lives of His saints.

In this volume, Roberts delineates and discusses the great principles of success which he has gleaned from the spiritual giants of the past. These are eternal principles — they will work in my life and in your life. Follow these principles — incorporate them into your lifestyle — and you too can become a spiritual giant. Ignore them and your spiritual life will be anemic. Roberts Liardon has learned to stand on the shoulders of spiritual giants. In this volume he invites you to do the same.

Paul G. Chappell, Ph. D.
Academic Dean
Graduate School of Theology
Oral Roberts University
Tulsa, Oklahoma

PREFACE

God's Word says, **You will ALWAYS be at the top, never at the bottom** (Deuteronomy 28:13 NIV).

I didn't say that — God did. Can God lie? Of course not! So why is it that so many Christians walk around defeated in many areas of their lives? We shouldn't be walking in defeat. God doesn't want us to be defeated, that's for sure. He wants every one of us ON TOP of things, on top of life, victorious and successful in all that we do.

The main reason so many people aren't walking in the total victory that God has for them is because they haven't truly seen success through *God's* eyes. There are many success books on the market today, but you will find this book drastically different from all the rest. It is not a book based on positive thinking or psychological tinkering to build your self-esteem; it is based on the Word of God. What makes it so different from all other success books you might read is that it contains THE TRUTH. It is not a compilation of a bunch of theories that have been tried and tested by behavioral scientists. This book has been tried and tested by God! His Word never fails. It always succeeds.

I've not written this book to help make you feel better about yourself. It's not the key to overnight success in ten easy steps. I want to help you see success the way God sees it, not the ways the world dictates. The ways of the world and God's way of success are not the same. I wrote this book to change your life, to stimulate you to develop into the successful Christian that God created you to be. When you apply THE TRUTH, God's truth, to your life, you will succeed. That's what God wants.

Success is a difficult concept to define. It is often associated with material wealth, self-satisfaction, prestige, or something along those lines. None of this is real success. We've all heard the stories of people who have everything they ever wanted, but they're still miserable. It's not what you get or have that makes you successful. It's who you are. When you are the person God created you to be, following His game plan for life, you cannot fail.

Let me tell you how this book came to be because it is supernatural. I had an encounter with Jesus when I was 11 years old. I was sitting in the living room watching television when all of a sudden Jesus walked in the front door. He came over and sat down on the couch next to me. I saw nothing but Jesus and His glory. His love engulfed me. Then He spoke to me:

"Roberts, study the lives of the generals in My great army. Know them like you know the back of your hand. Know why they succeeded and why they failed, and you'll want for nothing in this area of your life."

Then He got up and walked back out the door. Immediately I began to study great preachers throughout history. I read hundreds of books about such people as Smith Wigglesworth, Billy Sunday, Charles H. Spurgeon, Kathryn Kuhlman, John Alexander Dowie, John G. Lake, and many others. I interviewed their families and people who had worked with them or had known them; I collected tape recordings, films, pictures, diaries, and letters of these great men and women of God.

For six years I immersed myself in studying these people's failures and successes. I studied and studied and studied, just like Jesus told me to do. I found out why the great preachers throughout history succeeded and why some failed. It's important that we know why they succeeded and how they failed. The devil has nothing new under the sun. He has always been out to steal, kill, and destroy people's lives. This message exposes the traps the enemy sets for people's personal lives and for their ministries.

It's important that we be not ignorant of any of the devil's devices. God wants us to succeed at all we do for His honor and glory. The devil covers his traps with darkness, but the message of Light causes the darkness to flee. Whether a person has been a Christian for two months, two years, or twenty years, they can learn from the examples of God's generals.

When you understand how and why God's generals succeeded and failed, you will know what you must do to insure your own success. And we don't need more failures in the body of Christ today! Jesus is coming for a Church without spot or wrinkle. He wants every one of us to succeed.

Roberts Liardon
Tulsa, Oklahoma
October 1985

Chapter 1

Building on the Sure Foundation

Blessed is the man that walketh not in the counsel of the ungodly, nor standeth in the way of sinners, nor sitteth in the seat of the scornful.

But his delight is in the law of the Lord; and in his law doth he meditate day and night.

And he shall be like a tree planted by the rivers of water, that bringeth forth his fruit in his season; his leaf also shall not wither; and whatsoever he doeth shall prosper.

Psalm 1:1-3

The Word of God is our *sure* foundation. It is a foundation we can count on and one that does not fall apart in the face of adversity. Many people start off right — commiting their life to God and doing great things for Him — but halfway down the road they quit. Their world crumbles because they have not built their life or ministry on a good, strong foundation. If we stay on the *sure* foundation, we will *never* fail.

If you have ever been involved in the building process of a permanent structure, you know you can't have a solid home or building built on a weak foundation. If you build on a quickly laid, sloppy foundation, eventually it will slip and disaster will follow. You simply can't build your physical home on a mud slide and expect it to stay there. (Ask a Californian — they'll tell you that's true!) Likewise, you can't build your spiritual home on shifting sand. We must lay one brick at a time, and lay each one carefully.

Therefore whosoever heareth these sayings of mine, and doeth them, I will liken him unto a wise man, which built his house upon a rock:

And the rain descended, and the floods came, and the winds blew, and beat upon that house; and it fell not: for it was founded upon a rock.

And every one that heareth these sayings of mine, and doeth them not, shall be likened unto a foolish man, which built his house upon the sand:

And the rain descended, and the floods came, and the winds blew, and beat upon that house; and it fell: and great was the fall of it.

Matthew 7:24-27

If we build our spiritual life based on God's Word we will remain on the *sure* foundation. I want a foundation that is set correctly — one that is sure to stand, no matter what trials and tribulations come my way. Furthermore, you can't build a sure, strong foundation overnight. You can't climb God's ladder of success by hopping, skipping, and jumping three steps at a time. It takes time and perseverance. You have to put one foot in front of the other, taking one step at a time. That's the only way to build a foundation that will last.

Perfect timing also is involved in building a sure foundation. Construction workers know that concrete must be poured at a specific time, and you don't start building on top of it until it's firmly set. We need to stay in the perfect timing of God. If we're building our foundation on His Word, we'll not get ahead of God's timing. If we let God build our foundation, we can't go wrong.

GOD'S LOCAL CHURCH

And let us consider one another to provoke unto love and to good works:

Not forsaking the assembling of ourselves together, as the manner of some is; but exhorting one another: and so much the more, as ye see the day approaching.

Hebrews 10:24-25

One way to build a sure foundation is through the local church. God has set pastors over us to teach us the Word of God. We all need a pastor — someone in authority we can go to for counsel, and someone we can bounce our ideas around with. The Bible tells us there is wisdom in a multitude of counselors. (See Proverbs 11:14.)

We can't run from meeting to meeting or from church to church and expect to build a strong foundation. We've got to hook up with a local church body and attend regularly in order to mature properly. There's nothing wrong with attending special meetings, but believers who are always running here and there usually are unstable. Their doctrine and ideas are often different from what the Word teaches because they've not been under the discipleship of a pastor in a local church body. Only through consistent training and discipline in the local body will believers become the Church Jesus will return for.

GIFTS AND EXPERIENCES

That he might present it to himself a glorious church, not having spot, or wrinkle, or any such thing; but that it should be holy and without blemish.

Ephesians 5:27

Jesus wants a glorious Church without spot or wrinkle. Spots and wrinkles can be many different things: pride, jealousy, anger, and the like. But there's one particular spot or wrinkle in the Church that has caused great confusion. It's what I call *rocket believers* or *rocket preachers*. Such believers are people with no foundation.

Rocket believers start the Christian walk, zoom to fame and popularity overnight, then disappear just as suddenly as they appeared never to be seen or heard from again. Just like rockets they make a lot of noise, zoom up, and disappear into thin air! Another term for these kind of believers are roller-coaster Christians — up one day and down the next.

God doesn't want us to be rocket or roller-coaster Christians. He wants us to live in the high places with Him all the time, and when we do, our success is guaranteed.

God is my strength and power: and he maketh my way perfect.

He maketh my feet like hinds' feet: and setteth me upon my high places.

2 Samuel 22:33-34

One reason why believers and preachers don't walk in God's high places and don't live successful daily lives is because they have not built their lives or ministries on the sure foundation of God's Word. *When you build your life on God's sure foundation, you will not fail.*

This book of the law shall not depart out of thy mouth; but thou shalt meditate therein day and night, that thou mayest observe to do according to all that is written therein: for then thou shalt make thy way prosperous, and then thou shalt have good success.

Joshua 1:8

Stay in the Word of God, meditate in it day and night, obey its commands, and you are guaranteed success! Your life will be prosperous. This is not man's guarantee or a "money-back guarantee if not fully satisfied." This is God's guarantee. God's Word works when we apply it to our lives!

Another reason people fail to build a strong foundation is because they are looking to spiritual gifts and relying on spiritual experiences. People will fail if they try to build their lives on a spiritual gift or experience. Spiritual experiences are good when the Holy Spirit leads, but you can't build your life on them.

It would be easy for me to try to build my ministry on the trip I made to heaven when I was eight years old because everyone is always asking about it. I could have a big ministry in a few months' time based on that one story, but it wouldn't last. After a while, everyone would get tired of hearing about it. It was an experience that means a lot to me, but how would it benefit others? It would be my attempt at promoting myself and my ministry rather than letting God do the promoting.

You also cannot build a lasting ministry on some new revelation. There aren't any new revelations! **What has been will be again, what has been done will be done again; there is nothing new under the sun** (Ecclesiastes 1:9 NIV). Live in the constant revelation of God and His Word. Don't seek something wild and different to draw people or to impress people. That kind of thinking won't hold you when the storms of life hit.

I have read many books and magazines that were not written by the leading of the Holy Spirit. Some ministers have skillfully promoted themselves. They have built big ministries with many loyal followers. Yes, they have truth to give out, but when the tests and trials come, they are destroyed. Their poor foundation fails them.

We are not to be like that! We are not to build our lives or ministries on a spiritual experience, a spiritual gift, or a so-called revelation. We are to build our foundation on the *sure* foundation — God's Word.

The grass withereth, the flower fadeth: but the word of our God shall stand for ever.

Isaiah 40:8

Years ago during the great Voice of Healing days, many healing ministries flourished, but not many remain today. Back then, if you could just get to one of those meetings you would get healed. When the healing revival ended, almost all of those ministries collapsed, never to be heard from again. Why? Because their ministries were built on a spiritual gift — the gift of healing — rather than the *sure* foundation of God's Word.

When you begin to take your eyes off Jesus and His Word and look to something or someone else, you are headed for failure. You've got to keep your eyes on Jesus Christ and not let the things of this world get between you and God's Word. Some people put their trust in the paycheck they get every week. Others put their trust in other people, their reputation, or their education. All of those things are subject to change. The only thing that never changes is God and His Word.

> **For ever, O Lord, thy word is settled in heaven.**
>
> Psalm 119:89

I remember putting my trust in someone else for a time, and I was badly disappointed. One night I was in Hicksville, USA, crying out to God about it. I had finished ministering, and was alone in my hotel room. I laid on the floor crying out to God, "God, You left me."

He said right back, "No, I didn't. You left Me!"

"I did?" I asked. "What's the problem? When I preach, there's no power anymore. When I talk, nothing comes out of my mouth but skinny words. You know I like fat words full of power. What's wrong, God?"

The Lord told me I was putting my trust in other people and not in Him. It was causing me all kinds of worry because the people were changing on me. People change, but God doesn't. He changes not. The foundation of God — His Word — is sure. Nothing else around you may be sure, but He is.

> **Some boast in chariots, and some in horses; but we will boast in the name of the Lord, our God.**
>
> **They have bowed down and fallen; but we have risen and stood upright.**
>
> Psalm 20:7-8 NASB

You can stand upright at all times. When you are facing problems, don't run to the world. Don't run to natural solutions.

Don't run to some deep, new revelation, experience, or gift. Run to the Rock! Run to the *only* foundation that is sure. Run to Jesus and His Word!

Many times people fall apart when trials and tests come. When they try to put their troubled lives back together, they find they can't. If you get into the Bible and stay there, you will never fall apart. Your world might seem like it's falling apart all around you, but you will stand. If you have built your life and ministry on the sure foundation, you will never fail.

Run to the Rock of Jesus Christ. He has never cracked. He has never faltered. He's always been there. Rest and stand on that Rock. The Word of God is where you belong. It's where you need to put your trust. The Word works and is your key to success, whether it is the written Word or the Word spoken to your spirit.

Man shall not live by bread alone, but by every word that proceedeth out of the mouth of God.

Matthew 4:4

OBEYING GOD'S WORD

The Word of God rules supreme in successful believers' lives. They obey it without question. There was such a man in nineteenth century America. Peter Cartwright, a circuit-riding preacher, traveled from town to town preaching in little country churches. He obeyed God's Word without question, and one of his strongly held Methodist beliefs was that dancing was a terrible sin.

One day Peter preached in a certain town that was notorious for its big saloon. In those days, the saloons also housed the inn. Peter didn't like saloons, for not only did he preach against dancing, he also preached a strong message against alcohol and its evils. Usually, he would refuse to spend the night in any saloon if rooms were available elsewhere. But this night, there were no other rooms in town so Peter had to rent a room in the inn.

As Peter was getting settled into his room, a big dance got underway downstairs. He could hear the people below him milling about. Now Peter Cartwright loved all people — lost or saved. Although he could have stayed in his room and prayed, he was supernaturally drawn to the people downstairs. Love compelled him to reach out to them.

Peter walked downstairs and watched the people dance. The Spirit of the Lord spoke to him saying, "Peter, go dance with that young lady."

Peter almost fainted. He replied, "Lord, that's unthinkable! You know I can't do that! That's sin!"

But again the Lord spoke to him, "Go dance with that young lady." Even though Peter was fully convinced in his heart that it would be sin for him to do that, he obeyed God.

He walked to the middle of the dance floor and asked the young lady to dance. She smiled at him and accepted. He quickly told her, "First, there's something I must tell you. I have this habit. Before I do anything, I pray." With that, he dropped to his knees right there in front of her, surrounded by all the other couples dancing around them. He prayed fervently — and went on praying and praying and praying.

Suddenly, Peter's partner was slain in the spirit. Peter kept right on praying. Then he heard "ker-plop, ker-plop." He looked up. Couples were falling under the power of God all around him. Not one person was left standing. Everyone, including all the musicians, was slain by the Spirit of God.

Peter got up off his knees and began to preach. No one could get off the floor. They had no choice but to listen to him! It is recorded in history that every person in that inn was born again that very day! One man dared to be obedient to the voice of God, no matter what the cost, no matter what the circumstances dictated, no matter what his head said, and no matter what anyone else said of him. He chose to obey God.

Peter Cartwright's testimony of obedience to God is a success story. Successful Christians build their lives on the sure foundation and obey God's written and spoken Word. They know that whatever God tells them to do, He has given them the ability to do it, and whether it agrees with what they've been taught or not, they must obey Him.

Meditate in God's Word day and night and you too shall have "good success."

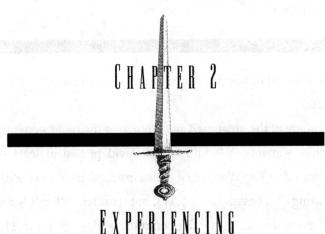

CHAPTER 2

EXPERIENCING
THE GLORY WORLD

The effectual fervent prayer of a righteous man availeth much.

James 5:16

People who walk in obedience to God's Word have something else going for them — a strong, consistent prayer life. Prayer is vitally important to our spiritual strength.

But ye, beloved, building up yourselves on your most holy faith, praying in the Holy Ghost,

Keep yourselves in the love of God, looking for the mercy of our Lord Jesus Christ unto eternal life.

Jude 20-21

People succeed with prayer. It does avail much and it changes things. It changes bad situations to the glory of God. Circumstances that look like they are going to do us in, all of a sudden turn out for our benefit. (See Romans 8:28.)

Many of the great men and women of the Bible were mighty prayer warriors. We know that David prayed at least three times a day. The Word of God also instructs us to **pray without ceasing** (1 Thessalonians 5:17), but it's often difficult for most believers to set aside five minutes a day to pray. There's something wrong with a believer who doesn't enjoy the power of prayer and the opportunity to talk to their Creator. When your prayer life starts declining, other areas of your life will start declining. Prayer is the only way you'll get to know the Father and the only way you'll get the power of heaven into your life.

There are men and women throughout history who were successful until they quit praying. When they quit praying, they got their eyes off of God, they lost their power, and they ended up someplace they shouldn't have been, doing something they shouldn't have been doing. Samson is a good example of this. When he got his eyes off of God, he fell.

TIME WITH GOD

We all need God's power in our daily lives and ministries. However, there's a price to pay to get that power, and it is spending time with God in prayer. The only way we can hook up with God's power is to spend time on our knees in communion with our heavenly Father.

I used to tell people to pray at least fifteen minutes a day. One time when I was preaching that, the Spirit of God corrected me. He told me to tell them that wasn't long enough. So I began to preach, "Pray thirty minutes." Then I upped it to an hour. When I said that, people choked and said, "Are you crazy? I can't pray an hour a day. I'm much too busy."

If you're too busy to pray and talk with your Father, you need to re-evaluate your priorities, because you are only cheating yourself. You won't have the power in your life that God wants you to have. Get up earlier, if necessary, to pray. Some people say, "But I need my sleep." You need God more than you need your sleep! Besides, when you get God's power generating in your body, you'll need less sleep, not more.

God is calling us to a supernatural realm of prayer and power. Sometime ago I asked the Lord about this and He said, "The only way you're going to find out about power is to get on your knees and come away with Me."

ACCESSING GOD'S POWER

There's another world out there that many men and women have never experienced — the glory world of God's power. In times gone by, there have been a few people who have tapped into this power, but very few. Not many want to pay the price of prayer to get God's power. But God is calling the whole Church — every believer — into this realm of power. He wants us to walk in that power to manifest His glory fully on the earth. He said His glory would fill all the earth and He wants to do that through us.

God wants us to walk in the fullness of His power so when we see a sick person, we can walk up to him and say, "Be made whole," and instantly the sick person is healed. When Jesus walked on the scene, devils screamed and departed and diseases left people's bodies. The sick and demon-possessed were instantly made whole. We often wonder why we don't see such things today in the Church. I believe it is because God's people are not spending enough time in prayer.

You cannot *confess* the power of God into your life. You can't walk around saying, "I have power. I have power." You can't plug into God's power just by quoting a few memory scriptures. All you'll get is a tired mouth! There is a higher realm than that, and the only way you can enter into that supernatural realm is by spending time on your hands and knees before Almighty God.

Long seasons of prayer are necessary so you can get out of your natural mind and into the spiritual realm. I call it "traveling with God in the realm of the glory world." It's possible, but it is done in the spirit, not in the flesh. Five minutes isn't long enough. If you spent only five minutes a day with your child, he wouldn't know you very well and you wouldn't know him very well, either. Your influence on that child would be minimal. It's the same with knowing God. You've got to spend lots of time with Him.

Be careful not to get caught up in a lot of grunting, groaning, and travailing because it's the popular thing to do. If the Holy Spirit is not moving on you to do it, then it's the flesh. God does not respond to fleshly prayers. True prayer and true intercession come by falling down on your face before God and seeking Him with your whole heart.

FIGHTING SPIRITUAL BATTLES

God is calling every one of us to move into the realm of the Spirit to do battle. It's time to quit operating in the flesh and start operating by the power of the Holy Spirit. Praying in tongues crosses us over from the flesh into the realm of the Spirit. Time becomes irrelevant. The only thing that will concern you is pressing on and getting closer to God.

Praying in tongues is so important because the natural mind has no spiritual power. It's the Holy Spirit in you who causes the devil to flee. Demons fight tongues like crazy because they know praying in tongues is our hotline to God. No demon can prevent a prayer in tongues from reaching the throne room of God. A prayer in tongues is spoken out of your spirit, and your spirit has power — the power of the Holy Spirit. The devil knows that, so he deceives people about tongues. However, it's one of the greatest weapons the Christian has.

When you don't know what to pray, pray in tongues. The Holy Spirit always knows what to pray. When you start praying in tongues, the answer is on the way and the devil is on the run! You will put devils to flight as you move over into the realm of the Spirit. There are a lot of spiritual battles going on in the world, and they must be fought with prayer. The Lord once said to me, "I need believers who will go out in the realm of the Spirit and fight." He said, "Angels can lose if there are not believers in the battle too."

God is calling us to get our lives straight and do what we need to do to go out and win the battle. He wants us to walk and talk with Him as a personal friend. He is calling us to separate ourselves unto prayer. The only way we'll ever experience God and His glory world is by staying on our faces before Him.

People ask me if I believe in seeing angels. I certainly do. They ask me if I believe in seeing devils. I certainly do. And do I believe in going into spiritual battle? I certainly do. I backed off from saying these things for a long time because I didn't want people to think I was strange. I finally decided it didn't make any difference what people thought. I had to preach what I knew to be the truth and God would take care of the people who think I'm strange, just as He takes care of me.

When I flew into Zimbabwe in 1984, God showed me a spiritual battle going on in that African nation and He said, "If believers don't fall on their faces and start praying for the nations, the nations are going to fall to the devil." Nations will fall if we don't pray!

I exhort therefore, that, first of all, supplications, prayers, intercessions, and giving of thanks, be made for all men;

For kings, and for all that are in authority; that we may lead a quiet and peaceable life in all godliness and honesty.

1 Timothy 2:1-2

We have a responsibility to pray for this world. Let's quit playing games and get into the midst of the spiritual battle and do warfare. Let's get serious with God. Let's get real. God has called us to this spiritual battle. Let's do what He has called us to do.

If we don't pray, this world isn't going to make it, and we won't make it in our own lives and ministries. I don't care how much knowledge we might have of the Word of God. I don't care if we are Greek or Hebrew scholars. I don't care how influential we might be. If we quit praying, we're headed for defeat!

PREVAILING PRAYER

My grandmother once said, "If you're going to be a success in life, you're going to have to know how to pray." She made me pray. She didn't ask me if I wanted to, she just said, "Pray," so I did. Prayer gives you power.

You'll be no greater than your prayer life. Prayer is the key to having God's power in your life. I'm not talking about little prayers that say, "God bless me," then end by quoting a couple of scriptures. I'm talking about a different kind of prayer — a prayer that prevails. Prevailing prayer does not give up until heaven and earth move to cause what needs to come to pass. Many times when God promises something, you're going to have to pray to get some movement going. God is not slack concerning His promises, but sometimes you've got to let God know you want His promises for your life. Elijah knew what prevailing prayer meant:

So Ahab went up to eat and to drink. And Elijah went up to the top of Carmel; and he cast himself down upon the earth, and put his face between his knees,

And said to his servant, Go up now, look toward the sea. And he went up, and looked, and said, There is nothing. And he said, Go again seven times.

And it came to pass at the seventh time, that he said, Behold, there ariseth a little cloud out of the sea, like a man's hand. And he said, Go up, say unto Ahab, Prepare thy chariot, and get thee down, that the rain stop thee not.

And it came to pass in the mean while, that the heaven was black with clouds and wind, and there was a great rain. And Ahab rode, and went to Jezreel.

And the hand of the Lord was on Elijah; and he girded up his loins, and ran before Ahab to the entrance of Jezreel.

1 Kings 18:42-46

Elijah did just that. While Ahab was eating and drinking, like most natural, carnal people do, Elijah, the prophet of God, spent time on his knees before God in prayer.

Elias was a man subject to like passions as we are, and he prayed earnestly that it might not rain: and it rained not on the earth by the space of three years and six months.

And he prayed again, and the heaven gave rain, and the earth brought forth her fruit.

James 5:17-18

Elijah prayed earnestly to stop the rain. Then he prayed earnestly to get the rain started again. Each time God answered his prayers. In developing a relationship with God, you're going to have to do some earnest praying to let God know you mean business and you really want His promises in your life.

Call unto me, and I will answer thee, and shew thee great and mighty things, which thou knowest not.

Jeremiah 33:3

That's exciting to think about! If we call on God's name, He'll answer us and show us great and mighty things we don't know about yet. I like that! Sometimes when I go into meetings, I just call on God. He answers. He shows up. He does what He says in His Word. We must pray to make it in life. Pray, pray, pray!

DANIEL — A MAN OF PRAYER

Daniel's name is synonymous with the word "prayer." He lived a life of prayer. When people talk about Daniel they talk about prayer. We need more Daniels today. Every preacher and every believer should be a Daniel because he was a man of great wisdom and knowledge. It came from his prayer life.

When we pray, God imparts wisdom and knowledge to our spirit man, not to our natural man. We might not understand all that is going on with our natural mind, but our spirit will have enough sense to follow the plan God gives us.

Daniel had an excellent spirit. He was able to discern spirits and interpret dreams. The king began to notice him and promoted him in the kingdom. (See Daniel 2:48.) God exalted Daniel to a high position; Daniel did not promote himself.

Humble yourselves therefore under the mighty hand of God, that he may exalt you in due time.

1 Peter 5:6

God knows where to put you when you humble yourself in prayer. People who don't pray don't get anywhere. That's why they're always trying to start something. You've got to "birth" your ministry in your prayer life before you start walking in it. And *you* must be the one to do it. You can't depend on someone else to pray your ministry through. The prayers of others will benefit you, but the ultimate responsibility rests on you. *You* are the one called to do the ministry God has set before you. You are the one God has anointed as its leader. Pray about it. It's your responsibility to do what He has told you to do.

Some in the king's government were jealous of Daniel. They didn't like Daniel having authority over them, so they decided to try to find something to cause Daniel's downfall.

> **Then said these men, We shall not find any occasion against this Daniel, except we find it against him concerning the law of his God.**
>
> **Daniel 6:5**

That's a good report right there. How would you like that to be said of you? If your enemies can say that about you, you're doing well! Daniel's enemies couldn't find anything wrong with him, so they tricked the king into signing a law stating that people were to pray only to the king, not to any god or person. (See Daniel 6:7-8.)

> **Now when Daniel knew that the writing was signed, he went into his house; and his windows being open in his chamber toward Jerusalem, he kneeled upon his knees three times a day, and prayed, and gave thanks before his God as he did aforetime.**
>
> **Daniel 6:10**

If you knew you would be persecuted for praying and then thrown into a lions' den if you were caught, would you pray as usual? Daniel did. As soon as the king signed that decree, Daniel said, "That's not going to stop me, and to prove it, I'm going to pray openly." He prayed, trusted in God, and was protected. We can learn much from Daniel's prayer life.

First, he committed himself to pray three times a day.

Secondly, he had set times that he prayed. He did not break those times, no matter what. He was a very busy man, but when it was time to pray, he stopped whatever he was doing and prayed.

Thirdly, as a result of his staying in God's presence in prayer, he was protected.

And when he had come near the den to Daniel, he [the king] cried out with a troubled voice. The king spoke and said to Daniel, "Daniel, servant of the living God, has your God, whom you constantly serve, been able to deliver you from the lions?"

Then Daniel spoke to the king, "O king, live forever!

"My God sent His angel and shut the lions' mouths, and they have not harmed me, inasmuch as I was found innocent before Him; and also toward you, O king, I have committed no crime."

Daniel 6:20-22 NASB (author's insert)

COMMITTING TO PRAY

If you have a set time to pray each day and you honor it, God will meet you there. He'll know He can depend on you to be there. If you have to get out of bed in the middle of the night to spend time with God in prayer, do it. Prayer is that important. Commit yourself to prayer and stick with it. Don't give up. If the going gets rough in prayer, stay at it a little longer. Some people tell me, "When I pray, my mind wanders." When your mind wanders, click it off and tell it to be quiet. You can take authority over your thoughts.

> Casting down imaginations, and every high thing that exalteth itself against the knowledge of God, and bringing into captivity every thought to the obedience of Christ.
>
> 2 Corinthians 10:5

When it is time for me to pray, my mind either shuts up or it agrees. I don't give it any other choices. You can control your total man. Tell your natural man what to do — especially during times of prayer because that is when God is moving. Nothing should get in the way of prayer. That is your priority. I don't care how often the doorbell rings, if you're praying, don't answer the door. I don't care how often the phone rings — don't answer it. If you're in prayer, stay there. Don't let anyone or anything pull you away from Jesus. When you mean business with the King, He'll do business with you.

Another mistake people make in their prayer time is they quit praying when the power hits. That is the time to *increase* your prayer time. That is the time to gain strength and take more ground in the spiritual realm.

When I was very little, my grandmother would tell my sister and me, "I'm praying. Come in here with me until I'm done." She would say, "I'm not coming out of this room until I've finished praying. If you die, I'm staying here." She would then shut the door, kneel down, and pray. My sister and I would sit there and play while she prayed. When we got older, we prayed too.

Many parents ask me what they should do with their children while they're praying. I tell them to take the children in the prayer closet with them. They are able to keep an eye on them while they are praying, and it is an excellent example to set before them. When children see that prayer is important to the parents, they will see it is important in their lives also.

Don't quit praying because circumstances dictate that it might not be a good time to pray. You rule the circumstances. It is up to you to impose God's spiritual laws on the natural.

When my sister and I got a little older, our grandmother let us out of the prayer room while she prayed, but she warned us, "Don't get hit by a car or anything while I'm in here praying because if you do, I'm not coming out! I'm not moving until I've finished praying!"

That was pretty stern, but it worked. She kept on praying, and she kept our lives safe. She kept us from getting seriously hurt. She kept us from the power of the devil. She went into her prayer closet, did battle with the enemy, and wouldn't give up until she had won. She would say, "I'm going to win or die trying!" That's what we need in prayer life — determination!

Elijah prayed earnestly that it might not rain, and it didn't. Then he prayed that it would rain, and it did. He got answers to his prayers because he was determined. He didn't pray a little tiny prayer and then get up and quit. He prayed until he got his answers.

Prevailing prayer works. We've got to have prevailing prayer in our lives as ministers and as believers. Prevailing prayer marches boldly into the throne room of God and stays there until it has received the mercy and grace needed to solve the problem. (See Hebrews 4:16.) Prevailing prayer blasts through mountains.

BLASTING THROUGH MOUNTAINS

Jesus answered and said unto them, Verily I say unto you, If ye have faith, and doubt not, ye shall not only do this which is done to the fig tree, but also if ye shall say unto this mountain, Be thou removed, and be thou cast into the sea; it shall be done.

And all things, whatsoever ye shall ask in prayer, believing, ye shall receive.

Matthew 21:21-22

It takes heavy equipment and powerful explosives to blast through a mountain, and it is the same with the mountains in your life. To blast through the problems in your life, you have got to use the powerful explosive material of prayer. You can blast your way through or you can drill your way through inch by inch. Some try to get around mountains by climbing over them. However, the mountain is still there. They have to face it again in the future if they don't destroy it.

Shortcuts in prayer won't work. You can't expect to have God's great power in your life by spending five minutes with Him here and there. You can't tackle something big if you haven't first dealt with smaller things. As my grandma used to say, "There are too many people trying to kill the giant when they haven't killed the lion or the bear first!" (See 1 Samuel 17:34-37.)

So blast through those mountains. Impose spiritual laws on the natural. Don't give in to the flesh. When you start blasting through mountains, you'll experience the death and burial of your flesh, and resurrection of your spirit. The death and burial of your flesh can be torture. Halfway through your mind will say, "Let's go back." But don't you dare go back! Keep on going. When you start this journey of prayer to conquer problems in your life, don't give up until you have been set free. I can't tell you how long it will take, but you'll know when freedom is yours. For some, it may take hours; for others, days. Some have more flesh that needs to die than others.

You must develop your own individual prayer life. You can't pattern your prayer life after that of others. Prayer warriors can only tell you their experiences. They can tell you how they got started, but they can't teach you how to enter into the presence of God. They can't teach you how to experience the glory of being in the Lord's presence. The Holy Spirit is the only one who can lead you into spiritual things.

The Bible never said to walk in the Spirit and the flesh at the same time. It never said to go in and out of the Spirit. It said to walk in the Spirit at all times. We can walk and live in the Spirit all the time.

And they that are Christ's have crucified the flesh with the affections and lusts.

If we live in the Spirit, let us also walk in the Spirit.

Galatians 5:24-25

The day I broke through, I thought heaven had come to earth. It was an inward excitement. Everything pertaining to this world fell away and I felt free. Mountain-moving faith was made available to me. I knew I could say to any mountain, "Move," and it had to move. It seemed there was nothing that could stop me. Every fear, doubt, and worry slipped away. I knew I had experienced the power of God.

We need to live in that kind of faith and power, and it comes through prayer. When you have that power from prayer in your life, you'll walk on the scene and things will change. Your presence will be so full of the power of God that people you come in contact with will be healed and saved. That is why people like Charles Finney could simply walk into a town and people would start crying out to God as he passed by. He lived in that glory world of God's constant, flowing power. When he walked into a room, things happened because he was filled with God's power, wisdom, and knowledge.

It is said that when Smith Wigglesworth would stand up to walk to the pulpit, a wave of power would sweep across the auditorium and people would be instantly healed — just because the man stood up! Now that's God's real power! Why did Wigglesworth have it? Because Smith Wigglesworth was dead to his flesh, and alive to the Spirit of God. When that body called Wigglesworth stood up, it wasn't he who stood up; it was Jesus in him. Wigglesworth knew what it was to live in the glory world, and he knew he had to crucify his flesh daily to live there.

That is what the world is looking for today. You must die to the flesh so the world can see Jesus in you, and prayer is the way you make it happen. There are no shortcuts. Let yourself die to the world, bury yourself, and keep blasting through that mountain to the other side, where your spirit man will rise up and soar in the things of God. You can go from glory to glory!

My goal is to live there all the time, and that is where God wants every believer to live. That is where Daniel lived. That is why he saw so many angels and why he knew so much about the Spirit realm.

Moses was another one who experienced the glory realm. When Moses walked up on the mountain, he had enough courage to walk into the cloud and commune with God. He came out with the glory of God all over him. He had to cover his face because his countenance was so bright the children of Israel could not look at him.

I imagine there were many times Moses wished he could have stayed up on Mount Sinai communing with God in the cloud, but God made him return to the people. In his absence they were doing strange things, including worshipping false gods. God said, "Go back and take care of them." God had a purpose and a plan for Moses to carry out, just like He does for you and me. When we spend time communing with God Almighty, we will know what those plans are and will be equipped to fulfill them. (See Jeremiah 29:11-13.)

The apostles also lived in the glory world. That is why people were healed when Peter's shadow fell on them as he walked by. God's glory heals people! Wouldn't it be nice if, when your shadow fell on people, they jumped up healed? It is possible. It's not something we can figure out with our natural minds, but it is possible in the spiritual realm.

If we were constantly walking in the Spirit, we would see such miracles happen more frequently today. God's glory is good, powerful, and liberating. It will set people free. But learning to move in the realm of the Spirit doesn't come naturally. It's something we learn as we spend time praying and meditating on the Word of God, learning the ways of the Holy Spirit.

THE POWER GENERATOR

A story is told about Aimee Semple McPherson's power. She was quite different from most Pentecostal women — and especially women preachers — in the 1930s and 1940s. She would say, "Who cares about all the do's and don'ts? I'm going to dress nice. I'm going to wear my wedding band. I'm going to put on lipstick." She did it too. She was a very attractive woman, and she got more people saved and healed in her meetings than most — in spite of the jewelry, makeup, and all. In some of her meetings, people on one whole side of a meeting hall would be slain in the Spirit.

Newspapermen wanted desperately to prove she was a fraud. One night, she was preaching in a big hall in Ohio and a reporter got a brilliant idea of how he could prove Aimee was a fake. He was convinced she was rigged with an electrical wire so that when she touched a person, it shocked them and knocked them out!

The reporter asked an usher, "Where's the power generator in this building?"

The ushers replied, "Oh, it's in the basement."

The reporter grabbed his trusty press camera and took off running for the basement. It was just the break he had been looking for! He ran to the basement door and flung it open. There before his eyes was the power generator — fifty little grandmas down on their knees praying! Prayer was Aimee's generator of power. Prayer power is what knocked those people off their feet.

It doesn't matter who you are — if you don't pray, your life will not be the way God intends it to be. You'll spend your days in the valley instead of on the mountaintop with God. You will find yourself constantly struggling with life's circumstances and trials because you'll be operating in your own power and not the power of God.

People of prayer spend hours on their knees before God. Smith Wigglesworth was such a person. God's power operated so strongly in his ministry that it totally astounded people. One time he walked up to a corpse, picked it up out of the coffin, and commanded life to come back into the body. The woman had been dead for three days, but he knew God's power could raise her from the dead. After he prayed, the woman opened her eyes and said, "Hello!" Now that's power!

A number of people were raised from the dead under Wigglesworth's ministry. This isn't something we should be surprised at because Jesus raised Lazarus from the dead, and He said we would do even greater things than He did! (See John 14:12.) The reason we're not seeing more of this mighty power of God operating today is because not enough power is being generated by prayer.

Kathryn Kuhlman was another great minister of God who walked in His power. She could stand in front of an audience and simply say, "Holy Spirit, move!" and people would pop out of wheelchairs all over the place.

Mile-long lines used to form outside of Oral Roberts' tent. People would wait for hours for that man to pray for them. The power of God was so strong on him that when people got next to him, they would begin to shake all over. Blind eyes would be opened, deaf ears would be unstopped, and the lame would jump up and walk. The altar calls were always full when Brother Roberts gave the invitation.

These great men and women didn't play games with God's power. They didn't think, *Well, God has called me, so I'll just walk out there in faith and the power will come.* No, that wasn't the key to their power. You can't walk out on the platform confessing power and expect it to show up. Power comes when you spend time on your knees in the presence of the Source of all power.

Those great preachers yielded themselves totally to the Spirit of God. They weren't afraid to do a few things in their prayer lives that might be a bit different. They allowed the Holy Spirit to flow through them.

Let the Holy Spirit enlarge your prayer language. Let the Holy Spirit flow through you in a new way today. There is a supernatural realm that the heart of God is longing for you to reach. He's calling you to go on with Him, to tap in to His power, and to explore His glory world. There is a deeper communion with God than you have known, but you won't get there unless you pray.

CHAPTER 3

GOD'S PLAN FOR YOU IS GOOD

"For I know the plans I have for you," declares
the Lord, "plans to prosper you and not to harm
you, plans to give you a hope and a future."

Jeremiah 29:11 NIV

God says to call out to Him and He will show us great
and mighty things which we know not. God has a
plan and a purpose for everyone's life. No person is
here on this earth by mistake. He created us for good
works — that people will see we are His handiwork
and then glorify our Father which is in heaven. (See
Ephesians 2:10.)

The reason so many Christians fail to achieve
anything in this life is because they never really find out
what God wants of them in the first place. Successful
Christians know they are an integral part of God's plan.

Where there is no vision, the people perish.

Proverbs 29:18

If we'll hook up with God's vision for our lives, we can't fail. One vision that every person should have is for lost souls to come into the kingdom of God. God will add to that vision, but you've got to start there. He will plant desires within your heart to accomplish His will on this earth.

Delight yourself in the Lord and he will give you the desires of your heart.

Psalm 37:4 NIV

Stay where God wants you to stay. Go where He wants you to go. Do what He wants you to do. Stick with the vision God gives you. Many believers and ministers received a vision from God and began to work toward fulfilling that vision, but somewhere along the line they got messed up. It became their vision, not God's. They started with God's ideas, but then added a few of their own. Soon, it was more their ideas than God's ideas. They began doing things on their own, claiming it was God who told them to do it. It won't work that way. Keep God's vision clearly before you. Don't muddy up the works with your own fancy ideas. None of your own ideas or your own works could ever outdo God's. If you want to see real results, do it His way.

When God tells you to do something, He always has perfect timing. If He says to do it now, you better do it now. If He says to wait, you better wait. His calling may not make sense to you at the time, but it will later on down the road. As time goes on, He will reveal His plans for you step by step.

When God called me at twelve years of age, one thing He told me I needed to do was study His generals. On March 18, 1984, I finished everything He had instructed me to do up to that point in my life. The last thing He had shown me to do was to preach in my home church. For the next two months, I didn't know what the next phase of His vision was for my ministry. But I didn't quit or give up during that time. I knew God had something more for me to do. Each new thing He asks of us will be bigger and better than the last. If we prove ourselves faithful in the little things, we will be granted much more. (See Luke 19:17.)

With each new set of new directions the Lord gives me, I have to put my full trust in Him. In the natural, sometimes the work seems impossible. My head tries to tell me I'm crazy for accepting the challenge. But I know God is a God of the impossible! (See Matthew 17:20.)

GOD OF THE IMPOSSIBLE

And Jesus looking upon them saith, With men it is impossible, but not with God: for with God all things are possible.

Mark 10:27

In order for you to accomplish the vision God has for your life, you must know that God is the God of the impossible. God specializes in impossibilities! There will be times when things look impossible to you. There will be times when you are tempted to quit. But if God said you can do it, YOU CAN DO IT!

But the people that do know their God shall be strong, and do exploits.

Daniel 11:32

Find out what God's vision is for you and go for it. Don't be worried about how it is going to happen because when He calls you, He equips you with everything you need.

You must first know that you are called. I knew the day I was first called into the ministry, and God sent someone along later to confirm it. The first person He sent was Kathryn Kuhlman. Now that was a miracle to me because I had admired her for so long. I had seen Catholic nuns get up out of wheelchairs in her meetings. In one meeting, a lady behind me was instantly healed of blindness and she began to scream, "I can see! I can see!" Those things made quite an impression on me!

When my mother graduated from Oral Roberts University, we had our photograph taken with Kathryn Kuhlman, who was the commencement speaker. Miss Kuhlman placed her thin hand on my head, tapped her little thumb on the top of my head and said, "You're going to be a preacher, aren't you?" She confirmed what God had already spoken to me. I just went on with what God had told me to do.

When the calling comes, be aware that devils will be assigned to try to talk you out of it. They will stick around and harass you until you let them know you mean business and you're going to answer the call no matter what. Protect your calling. It takes some people years to figure that out. Don't let the enemy steal it.

Many times, the call of God is known from the time a person is saved. It might not be accepted, but it's known. There were some days when I just didn't want to preach. I didn't want to be known as "the boy who saw heaven." I just wanted to be an anonymous teenager and live a normal teenage life.

The devil fought hard and tried to keep me from fulfilling the call of God on my life, but I couldn't get away from hearing Jesus' voice saying to me, "Go, go, go." There are some calls that are so vital to the body of Christ today that a person either obeys the call or dies!

Even though Paul was stoned, imprisoned, beaten, and shipwrecked, he never once wondered if he was saved, baptized with the Holy Spirit, or called by God — he just kept on going. When you have a call on your life, it's up to you to obey it. The apostle Paul knew beyond a shadow of a doubt that he was called. His encounter with Jesus on the road to Damascus changed his life forever. (See Acts 9:1-19.)

Then Agrippa said unto Paul, Thou art permitted to speak for thyself. Then Paul stretched forth the hand, and answered for himself:

I think myself happy, king Agrippa because I shall answer for myself this day before thee touching all the things whereof I am accused of the Jews:

Especially because I know thee to be expert in all customs and questions which are among the Jews: wherefore I beseech thee to hear me patiently.

My manner of life from my youth, which was at the first among mine own nation at Jerusalem, know all the Jews:

Which knew me from the beginning, if they would testify, that after the most straitest sect of our religion I lived a Pharisee.

And now I stand and am judged for the hope of the promise made of God unto our fathers:

Unto which promise our twelve tribes, instantly serving God day and night, hope to come. For which hope's sake, king Agrippa, I am accused of the Jews.

Why should it be thought a thing incredible with you, that God should raise the dead?

I verily thought with myself, that I ought to do many things contrary to the name of Jesus of Nazareth.

Which thing I also did in Jerusalem: and many of the saints did I shut up in prison, having received authority from the chief priests; and when they were put to death, I gave my voice against them.

And I punished them oft in every synagogue, and compelled them to blaspheme; and being exceedingly mad against them, I persecuted them even unto strange cities.

Whereupon as I went to Damascus with authority and commission from the chief priests,

At midday, O king, I saw in the way a light from heaven, above the brightness of the sun, shining round about me and them which journeyed with me.

And when we were all fallen to the earth, I heard a voice speaking unto me, and saying in the Hebrew tongue, Saul, Saul, why persecutest thou me? it is hard for thee to kick against the pricks.

And I said, Who art thou, Lord? And he said, I am Jesus whom thou persecutest.

But rise, and stand upon thy feet: for I have appeared unto thee for this purpose, to make thee a minister and a witness both of these things which thou hast seen, and of those things in the which I will appear unto thee;

Delivering thee from the people, and from the Gentiles, unto whom now I send thee.

To open their eyes, and to turn them from darkness to light, and from the power of Satan unto God, that they may receive forgiveness of sins, and inheritance among them which are sanctified by faith that is in me.

Whereupon, O king Agrippa, I was not disobedient unto the heavenly vision.

Acts 26:1-19

I like the first verse — **Paul stretched forth the hand, and answered for himself.** We have to speak for ourselves. We need to quit depending on other people to help us out. Never be in a rush when you are talking about the things of God and defending your life for Him. Be patient and take your time.

Paul knew his encounter with God was real and knew he was called. No one could talk him out of it. No matter what happened to him, knowing he was called kept him going. Sometimes it may be the *only* thing that keeps you going.

When you go out into the field, you must have that same type of knowing. You don't have to have the same type of visitation Paul had, but you can have an encounter with God. You will *know* you are called, and nothing will shake you from it.

As a young minister, I had responsibilities and pressures many older preachers do not have. As a teenager, it would have been easy for me to give up when the going got rough. I could have used the excuse, "Listen, I'm just a teenager. I can do what I want." But the truth was, I couldn't because I knew I was called.

When the enemy threw obstacles in my path, it would have been easy to sit down and start to wonder if fulfilling God's call was really worth it. The devil would sneak in with his crazy thoughts saying, "You're not really called. You're not supposed to be doing this now. You're too young anyway!" But I knew otherwise. I've known since the day Jesus said, "Go, go, go," that I was called.

When God spoke those three words to me, I realized I was called to preach whether anyone else was or not. Nothing can take that away from me. No matter how hard the circumstances get, no matter how hard the pressures get, and no matter what anyone says, I know I am called. I know God has a specific plan for me to fulfill.

When God calls you, He takes care of you. Don't worry about the circumstances. If you're walking in what you should walk in, and if you're doing what you should be doing, you'll do all right. If you're not despising the call, and if you're not trying to avoid the call, you'll do fine.

Some preachers have tried to run from the call of God on their lives. That's dangerous territory. Look what happened to Jonah when he ran from the call of God. You may not wind up in the belly of a great fish like Jonah did, but you might wind up in places that are worse! (See Jonah 1-2.)

When God calls you to do something, you can rest in the fact that He has already made the provisions for you to succeed. Power comes on you when you accept God's call. Dr. Lester Sumrall was a man of God who had a strong anointing on his life. At seventy years of age, he only slept a few hours every night! He was a constant, diligent worker, and with the call came the anointing and the power. The strong anointing affected his natural man with natural strength. A constant flow of God's anointing and power can come with the calling of God on your life, and there will be no stopping you.

ENCOUNTERING GOD

When Charles Finney was a lawyer, he didn't like God very much. He went to church basically for show and to prove to the people in his town what a good, moral person he was. He only wanted to live up to that day's standards for a good lawyer.

Finney didn't know God and wasn't interested in knowing Him. He attended a formal church and didn't find their presentation of God appealing. When people in the church would speak to him about getting saved, he would reply, "You folks pray like God is alive, but if He's real, why doesn't He ever answer your prayers? I don't want to get saved and give my life to God. I consider Him dead because He never does anything for you."

As hardened as Finney was, God had a way of getting his attention. God delights in taking those whose hearts are really hardened and turning their hearts toward Him. God wants sold-out people — ones who don't care what other people think. He wants people who dare to be different and enjoy it. Charles Finney was one of those men.

God used law to reach Finney. In some of his law books, Finney kept running across references to the Bible and to Old Testament laws. He finally bought a Bible to check out some of the references. When he began reading the Bible, the convicting power of God began to get hold of him.

He was very secretive about all of this. He didn't want anyone to know he was reading the Bible. If he heard someone coming, he would throw his Bible down and pile law books on top of it so no one would see what he had been reading. He finally got to the point where he would shut the door and plug up the keyhole with an old rag so no one would see him reading the Bible!

One day Finney was on the way to his office when the power of God hit him. He never made it to work that day. Instead, he went into the woods and got as far away from people as he could, found some logs that were heaped on top of each other, crawled under them, and began to whisper a prayer. He prayed, "O God, if You're really real, make Yourself known to me. Help me!"

Finney came out from under those logs a born-again Christian, ready to preach the Gospel, and ready to plead men's cases before God instead of in the courts of the land.

Finney went by his office and said, "I quit."

People asked him, "What are you going to do?"

Finney replied, "I'm going to preach."

Finney went to a nearby street corner, started preaching, and never stopped. He was called the greatest revivalist since the apostle Paul. He knew what it was to move in the power of prayer and to go into cities and destroy the devil.

Finney knew he was called from the time he was first saved. Some people ask me, "How will I really know I'm called?" If you don't know, you haven't had a real encounter with God yet because once you've truly been called, there's no room to wonder about it. When you come in contact with God, you know. Now the devil will try to convince you otherwise, or try to plant doubt in your mind. But always bring to remembrance the day you received God's calling.

Remember, therefore, what you have received and heard; obey it, and repent.

Revelation 3:3 NIV

BURDENED OR CALLED

If you are a preacher who is not sure you're called, you're on dangerous territory. You would be better off living in your prayer closet for awhile before you go out in the field. Too many preachers have entered the ministry wondering if they're called or not. They don't last. You must *know* you are called, then do what God has called you to do. For this reason, it is important to know the difference between a *burden* and a *call*. Many people see a need for something and they start things they never complete because they were never called to do it in the first place. If God has called you to do something, you'll finish it.

Some people go overseas thinking they're called to the mission field when they really just have a burden. They begin to build a school for the people, and halfway through when problems develop, they quit, run, and excuse themselves, saying, "God didn't call me to that." Either He did or He didn't! Which is it? We've got to get it straight. People's lives are at stake. People will be hurt by our actions if we're confused as to what God has called us to. With His calling comes a great responsibility to be faithful and to fulfill that calling.

People who don't finish things they start probably never were called in the first place. If they were, they obviously weren't faithful to the call. Chances are, they simply had a burden and there's nothing wrong with that. I get burdens about a lot of things. You should pray about burdens. You may want to offer financial support to help with some of those burdens. You even may want to give of your time in labor to it. But a burden is not a call.

Burdens generally last a short time. Calls last a long time — they last forever. A call is compelling. It burns within your heart. Your mind dwells on it. An inner voice constantly speaks to your spirit. If you want to know God's specific call on your life, pray and ask God to reveal it to you. Wait on Him and ask Him what He would have you do. He will tell you.

I have a friend who was called to be an evangelist shortly after she was saved. At the time, she was a newspaper reporter and the Lord used her in Christian writing for several years. But the call of God on her life compelled her to preach every chance she got. She began to preach frequently in prisons and small churches throughout the country, but she yearned to reach more and more lost people.

For years, she struggled with the call of God on her life. She had seen so many people who had gone into the ministry and failed, and she didn't want to follow in their footsteps. She began to pray earnestly about it, and the voice within her that kept telling her to reach multitudes was getting louder and louder.

One day she cried out to God, "I've got to know, God. I can't go on like this. This fire within my bones won't go away. Do I continue to write full-time and preach part-time or vice versa? Do You want me to devote my energies to full-time ministry? What do You want me to do?"

The Lord instructed her to attend a meeting later that week and she would get her answer there. At that meeting, a prophet of God picked her out from the crowd and said, "The Lord told me to tell you this. 'Know this, you are called. Don't ever question it again. That is sin. He has called you, and He will use you mightily. Watch as He opens many doors for you this year.'" Within six months, she was in full-time ministry and now serves as a missionary overseas. She has traveled to more than a dozen countries proclaiming God's Good News to multitudes of lost souls.

Get God's vision and call for your life established in your heart like my friend did, and you can't fail. God has success for you!

TURN STUMBLING BLOCKS INTO STEPPINGSTONES

Challenges do come with the call. Expect them! Successful believers and successful ministers are not afraid of challenges. They look at challenges and problems as steppingstones rather than stumbling blocks. They never let problems become excuses to give up and quit. But many believers and ministers fail because they allow problems to shipwreck them.

> My brethren, count it all joy when ye fall into divers temptations;
>
> Knowing this, that the trying of your faith worketh patience.
>
> But let patience have her perfect work, that ye may be perfect and entire, wanting nothing.
>
> James 1:2-4

Challenges and problems come in all shapes and sizes. Life is full of them. You can't be victorious by running from them. You must deal with them and learn from them. You profit by facing challenges, problems, and mistakes squarely. Although our nature is to rationalize things away if we can, in doing so, we only lose. We succeed, however, if we face the challenge and learn from it.

William Branham is a good example of someone who stared challenges down. Once when he was ministering in Africa, all the witch doctors were mad at him because their businesses were going broke. People who used to go to the witch doctors were now going to Branham's meetings and getting healed — free of charge!

The witch doctors got so upset about it they sent Branham a letter warning him they were going to destroy him. They were going to cause a storm to come and kill him during one of his meetings. Branham went on with the meeting. He never let it faze him, even though storm bulletins were posted and the threat was very real.

Fourteen witch doctors showed up at that meeting, surrounding Branham's tent. The storm came up just like they predicted. Some people got worried and tried to convince Brother Branham to leave, saying, "Mr. Branham, we've got to get you out of here. Those witch doctors aren't fooling around. They mean business. That storm is destroying everything in its path!"

Branham politely responded, "I come in the name of the Lord. I don't need to be afraid of anything or anyone. God will protect me."

Branham knew God had called him to that part of Africa and nothing was going to stop him from doing God's work. The storm came to the edge of the tent, but Brother Branham stood there and prayed, "Father, protect us." He bound the evil spirits and the storm detoured around the tent! The canvas didn't even shake in the wind. There was total peace inside because of one man's prayers. He didn't allow the challenge to overcome him. He faced it and refused to let it get him down. They had a revival that night, you can be sure!

Trust God to pull you through any challenge you face. Our God is a big God. He can take care of all our problems, big or small.

A SPIRIT OF PERSISTENCE

Along with facing challenges, successful Christians know what it means to be persistent. I call it having a *persistent spirit*.

They use persistence in a profitable manner. I say in a profitable manner because some use it in an unprofitable manner. Some get pushy and demand things that are unreasonable of other people, but that is not what I am talking about.

Persistence, perseverance, or stick-to-itiveness is a necessary quality to be successful. With a persistent spirit, you can face challenges and hold on to the vision God has given you, bringing it to manifestation. Persistence is a test of faith. Persistence is hanging in there when all the odds are stacked against you. It is steadfastness.

John G. Lake was a man who was persistent. He built and directed a Bible school in Spokane, Washington. He used to say to his students, "We're going to give each of you the name of a sick person. They need prayer. You are to go to them and pray for them to be healed. Don't come back until they are healed. If you do, you'll have to deal with me!"

Lake's boldness was motivated by love. Perfect love casts out all fear. (See 1 John 4:18.) He loved people so much that he wanted to see everyone healthy, whole, and walking in all of God's blessings.

Some of those students prayed half an hour. Others would stay all day to pray for a sick person. Some even stayed two weeks! But they did not return to school until the person was totally healed. That's persistence. When persistence is fueled by love — God's love for people — you will succeed.

Therefore, my dear brothers, stand firm. Let nothing move you. Always give yourselves fully to the work of the Lord, because you know that your labor in the Lord is not in vain.

1 Corinthians 15:58 NIV

CHAPTER 4

POSSESSED WITH GOD'S LOVE FOR PEOPLE

Love never fails.

1 Corinthians 13:8 NIV

Successful people walk in love at all times, no matter what happens. We must *choose* to walk in love. It is a choice. Love for people doesn't just overtake us when we become born again, but when we fully realize the love God has for us and see others the way He sees them, we can walk in His love.

Dear children, let us not love with words or tongue but with actions and in truth.

1 John 3:18 NIV

Love is action. Love will compel you to reach out to the lost. It will make you go where the sinners are. Sinners aren't inside the church — they're outside the church. That's where you need to go. Love will make you run to the valley of the shadow of death to get someone and bring them to the mountaintop of God.

Love has compelled me to reach out to people since I was a young boy. I first got started in the ministry passing out witnessing tracts in different neighborhoods. God had called me to preach, but no churches were giving me speaking invitations, so I went out and preached to everyone I could find on the street. I would walk down the street, hand someone a tract, and begin to weep.

"What's wrong?" the person would ask me. I would tell them I was sad because they didn't know what I knew. I told them how much God loved them, how He wanted to heal them, deliver them, and make them whole in every area of their lives.

I wasn't trying to manipulate them with false sincerity. I was truly grieved over the fact that they did not know Jesus and were not living the life God had intended for them. A lot of people came into the house of God because I let the compassion of Jesus flow through me to them. It was embarrassing to stand there and cry in front of someone I had never met before, but love made me do it! I made the choice to allow it to happen. I could have chosen to sit at home and watch television or do something else, but I chose to reach out to people in need. That's the love of God at work. What good does it do to tell people God loves them when we don't show that love?

Love meets the needs of people. When you meet someone who is sick, love compels you to lay hands on them and pray for them so they'll recover. If you're not walking in love, you'll just look at that sick person and say, "Oh dear, I'm so sorry you're sick." That's not enough. Love acts. The love of God sometimes will impress you to do things your natural mind rebels at. Your natural mind will say no, but the spirit of love will say yes.

There was a minister by the name of Jerry B. Walker who said he didn't have the love of God the way he felt he should, so he locked himself up for seven days and did nothing but pray. All he asked for was that the compassion of Jesus would fill him. When he walked out on the seventh day, the compassion of Jesus flowed out of that man. When he preached, you could feel God's love flowing out of him. That love drew all kinds of people into the kingdom of God. It moved the whole place because he let the love of Jesus flow through him.

It's time we all walked in such love. The operation of God in our lives must be characterized by love. That's the only way the world is going to be won. It's the only way the Church is going to survive.

And this is love: that we walk in obedience to his commands. As you have heard from the beginning, his command is that you walk in love.

2 John 6 NIV

Dear friends, let us love one another, for love comes from God. Everyone who loves has been born of God and knows God.

Whoever does not love does not know God, because God is love.

Dear friends, since God so loved us, we also ought to love one another.

No one has ever seen God; but if we love one another, God lives in us and his love is made complete in us.

1 John 4:7-8,11-12 NIV

The Christian army is one of the most unusual armies in the world. It is the only one I know of that kills its wounded. I'm serious! We kill by our words and actions. It's time we quit killing our wounded and started bandaging them up, loving them, and keeping the Church glorious.

It is sin not to stand by our fellow believers and ministers and support them when they are going through a rough time. In the natural world, doctors stand by other doctors; lawyers stand by lawyers; family members stand by family members. Why can't believers stand by other believers? Why can't ministers stand by fellow ministers?

David stood by King Saul even in death. When King Saul was dead, a man came running to David with the news that King Saul had committed suicide. David had every reason to rejoice because King Saul had been a major thorn in his flesh.

He had even tried to kill David more than once! Yet David cried bitterly because King Saul had died. Then he said, "Don't tell anyone. Don't publish this in Gath. Don't go to the other lands and tell them our king is dead, lest they rejoice. Let's keep it quiet." (See 2 Samuel 1:20.)

That is the way it should be in the Church and in ministry today. We shouldn't be publishing and broadcasting the failures of our brothers and sisters. If we want to concern ourselves with the affairs of others, it should be between us and God — on our hands and knees in prayer.

Church people love gossip probably more than any other people on the face of the earth. Some churches never grow because the members have sown so many bad seeds through their gossip. Some of the major hindrances to believers walking in love are strife, slander, and gossip. Strife among the brethren is a dangerous thing.

For where envying and strife is, there is confusion and every evil work.

James 3:16

We should not be the source of strife in any way in our home, church, or community. We should be the source of harmony, peace, unity, and love. We need to be in the S.O.S. business: Stamp Out Strife!

Let no corrupt communication proceed out of your mouth, but that which is good to the use of edifying, that it may minister grace unto the hearers.

And grieve not the holy Spirit of God, whereby ye are sealed unto the day of redemption.

Let all bitterness, and wrath, and anger, and clamour, and evil speaking, be put away from you, with all malice:

And be ye kind one to another, tenderhearted, forgiving one another, even as God for Christ's sake hath forgiven you.

Ephesians 4:29-32

Love does not run around the church telling everyone what you know about So-and-So. Love doesn't talk badly about church leadership. Love speaks good things. And if you can't say anything good about someone, go into your prayer closet and pray. If you see something that isn't quite right, love doesn't broadcast it all over the place, causing strife and division. Love prays and believes the best.

When strife is dealt with, power will come. But when there's strife and discord, all kinds of doors are opened up for the powers of darkness to come in. It is time we became the source of unity, love, faith, and power in our churches. Church splits are not of God. It's not God's plan for churches to split. God's love promotes unity. God's love brings people together; it doesn't separate.

Above all things have intense and unfailing love for one another, for love covers a multitude of sins — forgives and disregards the offenses of others.

1 Peter 4:8 AMP

> Love worketh no ill to his neighbour: therefore love
> is the fulfilling of the law.
>
> **Romans 13:10**

When we walk in love, we fulfill God's law. He told us to love Him with all our heart, mind, and soul, and to love our neighbor as ourselves. (See Luke 10:27.) Love will overlook any wrong anyone has ever done to us. Love forgives.

There's a big plus to walking in love. The body of Christ must make every effort to walk in God's love at all times because faith works by love. (See Galatians 5:6.) When we walk in love, we walk in great faith. Why is this? Because God is love.

When the compassion of Jesus combined with faith flows through us, we will do mighty exploits for Him. When Jesus saw the multitudes, He was moved with compassion to reach out to them and healings and miracles abounded. As He was, so are we to be in this world!

Kathryn Kuhlman once said, "You must believe in the religion of love. Love for everyone, everywhere — the rich and the poor, the learned and the unlearned, the well and the afflicted. That's the religion of love. It satisfies the heart. It's deep enough for the soul and broad enough for the whole world and everyone."

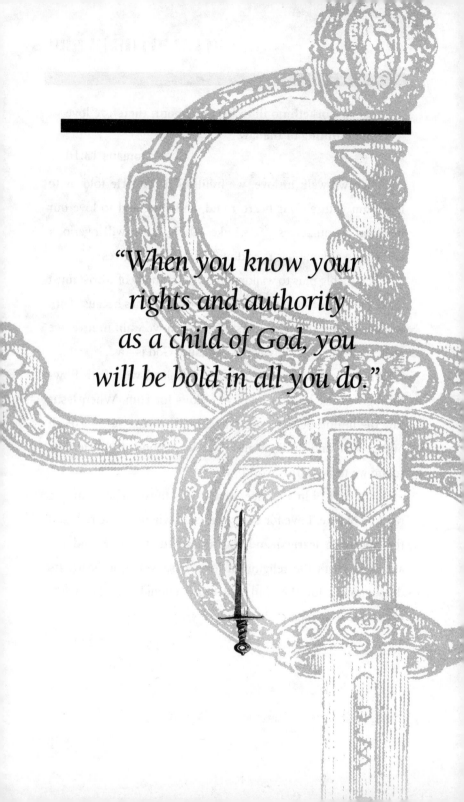

"When you know your
rights and authority
as a child of God, you
will be bold in all you do."

CHAPTER 5

BOLD AS LIONS

The righteous are bold as a lion.

Proverbs 28:1

Perfect love casts out all fear (see 1 John 4:18) and as we are perfected in God's love, supernatural boldness becomes a part of us. Successful Christians stare challenges in the face with holy boldness. They aren't afraid of problems. They look at them as stepping-stones to something better. On the other hand, those who look at problems as hindrances and let problems become excuses never succeed. Bold people walk right over the problems and go on to something bigger and better. Bold people walk in unshakable faith. People who are bold trust God to do what He has promised.

Jack Coe is an example of a bold preacher. He had strong faith in God, and when God said to do something, Coe did it automatically with no questions asked. He trusted God. One time, Coe lined up all the crippled people in his meeting. He walked over to the first man, grabbed him by the shirt, and threw him over his shoulder. He went down the line, picking everyone up and throwing them over his shoulder! Now from the natural standpoint, that would seem like a very odd thing to do. I don't know of any modern-day preachers who would make that part of their service. But in that very challenging situation, Jack Coe had heard from God and acted in obedience. As a result, every one of those crippled people was instantly healed!

Jack Coe accepted the challenge, boldly stared it in the face, and said, "God, let's get them healed." Coe would have been in deep trouble if that hadn't been God, but it was and he knew it. He was bold enough to do what God commanded him to do.

The people that do know their God shall be strong, and do exploits.

Daniel 11:32

Bold people know who they are in Christ. They know their rights. When you know your rights and authority as a child of God, you will be bold in all you do.

John G. Lake is another good example of boldness. He knew who his God was, and he knew the authority that was available to him. He proved this once in South Africa when the bubonic plague struck the area where he was ministering. He volunteered to help bury the dead and care for the living. When a relief ship finally arrived from England, the doctors wanted to give Lake some serum for protection because he had been in such close contact with the germs. Normally, such contact would prove fatal. Lake declined their offer saying he didn't need the serum. The doctors asked him what he meant and Lake boldly said, "I don't go by the natural law. I go by the law of Christ. The law of life lives in me, not death."

To prove his statement, Lake took some of the bloody foam from the lips of a plague victim and placed it in his hand. Then he stuck his hand under a microscope and said, "Those germs can't live on me. They must die." Sure enough, when the doctors looked under the microscope, the germs had all died on Lake's hand! He walked by God's divine law, not by the natural laws of this world. As a result, he walked in authority and boldness.

Another man who walked in great boldness was Smith Wigglesworth, who was an uneducated plumber when he got saved. His wife was actually the preacher when he got started, but as he went along, the power of God and the anointing of God caused Smith to be a great preacher. He was as bold as they come.

A man once came to him with a swollen stomach, complaining of kidney troubles and in a lot of pain. When he asked Smith to pray for him, Smith hauled off and punched the man right in the stomach. As soon as his fist hit the man, he was instantly healed! That's boldness! That's also obedience to God.

However, don't try something like that unless you know God has spoken to you to do it. You might just get hit back!

Paul prayed that he would speak the Word of God boldly. When you speak the Word of God boldly and with authority, people will listen. Not many people listen to mealy-mouthed Christians. We must be bold. The Bible says we're to be as bold as lions. You can't get much bolder than that!

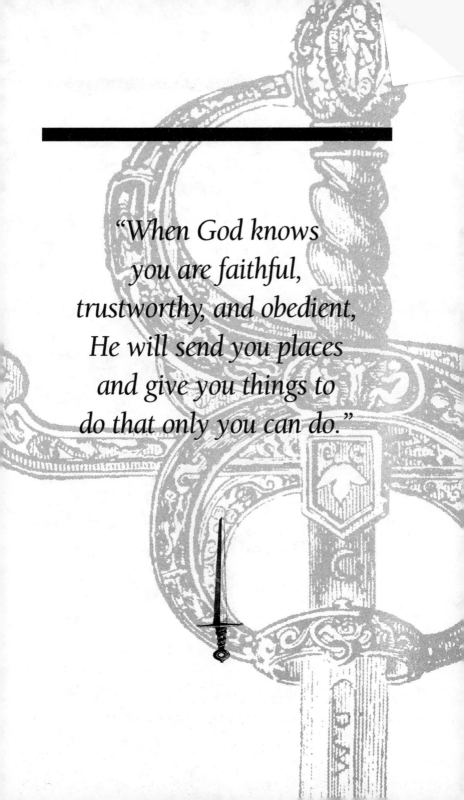

"When God knows
you are faithful,
trustworthy, and obedient,
He will send you places
and give you things to
do that only you can do."

CHAPTER 6

WALKING WITH GOD AT ALL TIMES

**Know ye not that ye are the temple of God,
and that the Spirit of God dwelleth in you?**
1 Corinthians 3:16

Successful Christians know the Trinity: God the
Father, God the Son, and God the Holy Spirit. When
you rely on the Trinity in all you do, your success is
assured. When you are totally dependent upon the
Trinity, you become aware of God's presence at all
times. You and God can walk together as friends every
day because He lives inside of you. A moment doesn't
go by that you are not aware of God being with you.

When you are aware of God's presence in your life,
you don't want to say or do anything that would bring
reproach on Him or would grieve the Spirit of God.
When you get up in the morning do you mumble, "Oh,

another day"? Or do you say, "Good morning, God. Good morning, Jesus. Good morning, Holy Spirit"?

When you go to bed at night, do you pray, "Father, bless me and no more," hop into bed, and go to sleep? Or do you say, "Good night, God. Good night, Jesus. Good night, Holy Spirit"?

SPIRIT-LED PEOPLE SUCCEED

The first thing Smith Wigglesworth did each morning was dance before the Lord for ten minutes, worshipping and praising God. Whether he felt like it or not, he did it to honor God and thank Him for a new day. He also wouldn't go for more than fifteen minutes without either reading God's Word or praying. If you were riding in a car with him and went past the fifteen-minute mark, he would yell, "STOP!" Then he would make everyone get out of the car, get on their knees, pray, and repent for ignoring God! That's how God-conscious he was. He was well aware that God the Father, God the Son, and God the Holy Spirit were walking with him every minute of every day.

Evan Roberts was another person who knew God like this. He lived in Wales at the turn of the century, and when he was just a little boy, he would get up early every morning and run to the coal mine in town with his "scorched Bible." It was called a scorched Bible because one time the mine exploded and burned some of his Bible.

Evan would be at the entrance to the coal mine waiting for the miners to come to work every morning. As they descended into the mine, he would read them a scripture verse. At the end of the day, he would be back at the mine again, waiting for the miners to come back up.

As they came out of the mine, he would ask them what they thought of the scripture for the day. Sometimes they would answer him. Sometimes they would hit him. But most of the time they would just laugh at him. Evan didn't care. He was aware of God's presence in his life and his boldness came from doing what he knew God wanted him to do.

Evan wasn't educated. He had no money or popularity, but when he was twenty-six years old, he told his pastor he was going to preach at the next youth service. The pastor said, "Well, very well." When the time came, Evan walked into Moriah Chapel, opened his little scorched Bible, and said this prayer: "Oh, Holy Spirit, bend us. Oh, Holy Spirit!"

Think about those words for a minute. They showed Evan's dependence on the Holy Spirit. They proved his consciousness of God. When those words were uttered, the Holy Spirit swooped in and knocked Evan to his knees in intercession. Then the Holy Spirit swept across the congregation. They all began to cry and weep in response to the Holy Spirit's conviction.

That started the Welsh Revival. During that time of revival, you couldn't find a sinner in the entire country of Wales. If you journeyed into the country a sinner, you would come out a Christian! The saloons all closed down. Prostitutes went home.

Everyone lived a holy life. The policemen were out of jobs because the populace didn't need their services anymore. Instead of the crusty miners cursing and drinking, they would walk down the streets praising God. They even had to retrain the little pit ponies in the mines to adjust to the miners' new, sanctified vocabulary!

The Welsh believers became conscious of God walking with them every day, they depended on the Holy Spirit, and they surrendered everything to God. These three things will bring you success.

Kathryn Kuhlman was another person who totally depended on the Holy Spirit. She was always aware of God's presence. Some people called her crazy because she walked around talking to God all the time. Others hounded her about the miracles that took place in her ministry.

She would tell them, "I'm absolutely dependent on the power of the Holy Spirit. I have stood before sick people and cried, wishing I could give them strength from my own body. But without the Holy Spirit, I have nothing — NOTHING!"

Miss Kuhlman gave her all to God. Before her services, she would pace backstage, weeping, telling God it wasn't her power, but His power that healed the people. It was a humbling sight. She often said, "The only fear I have is that when I walk out into a great miracle service, the presence of the Holy Spirit won't be there. I know I have no healing power. It must be the Holy Spirit's work. He must do it. I can't."

Kathryn Kuhlman was totally dependent on God the Father, God the Son, and God the Holy Spirit. She walked with them at all times.

GOOD MORNING, GOD!

When I came back from my visit to heaven, I yearned for the same closeness with Jesus I had enjoyed while I walked with Him on the streets of gold, so I began to seek a closer relationship with Him. How desirous are you of a close relationship with Jesus? How earnest are you? Faith doesn't give up until you get your answer. How much do you really want it? If you really want an answer, you'll not give up. You'll stick with it until you get your answer or see your miracle. Just don't let the devil gyp you out of all God has for you. Develop your relationship with God, Jesus, and the Holy Spirit.

God longs for people to want to be His friend. He created us so we could walk and talk with Him. God actually talked with Moses face to face.

And the Lord spake unto Moses face to face, as a man speaketh unto his friend.

Exodus 33:11

If Moses, Enoch, and Abraham could walk and talk with God and be His friends, so can we. Those men were great because they walked and talked with God as His friends. But we have to choose God at all times and serve Him in truth and sincerity.

A relationship with the Holy Spirit keeps you from getting in hot water. He will keep you in the middle of the road and out of the ruts on the left and right. You'll begin to know the heartbeat of God when you develop a relationship with Him. You'll learn of His character when you spend time in the Word. God is the most loving person I have ever come in contact with. Jesus is the most caring individual. He cares about us so much — enough to die for us.

The Holy Spirit is the most unique individual. He's always coming up with surprises. He's always doing something unexpected. Learn to be sensitive to the moving of the Spirit of God. In developing a relationship with Him, you'll know in your spirit when He's speaking to you — guiding, directing, and teaching.

I believe many people miss visitations from God because they are waiting for something to happen they can see or touch in the natural realm. It doesn't happen in the natural realm — it happens in the spiritual realm.

Every time I've had a visitation from God, I have picked it up in the spiritual realm long before I ever sensed anything in the natural realm. We must become Spirit-oriented people and not worry about the natural realm. The natural can find out about it later.

VICTORY EVERY TIME

If you are born again and the life and nature of God have become a part of you, you won't understand defeat. God does not understand defeat, so why should you? God never has known defeat. If you are led by the Holy Spirit, who is on the inside of you, He will lead you into victory every time. The only thing the Spirit understands is victory. He doesn't know what it is to lead people to defeat.

When I have missed it, I can tell you why I have missed it every time — I didn't listen to my spirit. My spirit was saying, "NO, NO, NO," and my head was saying, "YES, YES, YES." Is a war going on inside of you? Is your mind saying, "YES, YES, YES," but your spirit is saying, "NO, NO, NO?" You better listen to your spirit! Tell your mind to be quiet and listen to what the Spirit of God on the inside of you is trying to tell you.

How trustworthy are you in your relationship with God? God looks at the past and at the future. Have you been quick to obey Him in the past? Have you been faithful in the small things? When we develop a close relationship with the Father, He'll know we are trustworthy. When we request things of Him, He will grant them, but He's got to know we are trustworthy.

The gifts and calling of God are without repentance.

Romans 11:29

God will not take back what He has given to an individual, but if you don't use the gift God has given you or heed His calling, it will never become a completed work. God has called you because He knows you are capable of fulfilling that call. It is His investment in you. When you are faithful, trustworthy, and obedient, He will send you places and give you things to do that only you can do.

FRIENDS WITH GOD

God has always wanted us to walk with Him as friends. When God made Adam they became friends. God came down in the cool of the day, and He and Adam walked and talked together as one. They did everything together, but when Adam fell, their friendship was destroyed. Adam lost everything because of sin.

God found another man with whom He could walk and talk in Enoch. Enoch walked with God for three hundred years as God's friend. (See Genesis 5:22-24.) However, there were only two men who actually walked *with* God — Noah and Enoch. Abraham walked *before* God. (See Genesis 17:1.) There's a difference between walking before God and walking with God. Walking with God means walking shoulder to shoulder with Him. When we walk shoulder to shoulder with God, we are able to see into the realm of the spirit. The spirit realm is God's world and it is more real than anything else.

We can walk with God just like Enoch did, getting closer to Him each day. When you walk in the realm of the spirit and are conscious of God at all times, you will see and do things that might seem strange to everyone else around you, but that's a small price to pay for knowing God. It's worth it to be obedient to His Word and it's worth it to have that close, intimate relationship with the Father.

By faith Enoch was taken from this life, so that he did not experience death; he could not be found because God had taken him away. For before he was taken, he was commended as one who pleased God.

And without faith it is impossible to please God because anyone who comes to him must believe that he exists and that he rewards those who earnestly seek him.

Hebrews 11:5-6 NIV

If you had lived back in Enoch's time, you probably would have seen him talking into thin air much of the time, because Enoch had a relationship with God. Enoch's faith pleased God. Does your faith please God? Are you striving to have a relationship with God like Enoch had?

God is not so far off that we can't touch Him. He is not in some far away place that He can't hear our cries. He is on the inside of us, desiring us to walk and live by His Holy Spirit and to have constant communion with Him. Furthermore, your spirit man longs to walk with God as a friend. It's our head that gets in the way! It is our inner man of the heart who walks and talks with God.

We can be conscious of God at all times, but in order for this to happen, we've got to let our spirit man rule every area of our mind and body. The natural mind will rebel against the things of the Spirit because it's not accustomed to them. But the spirit man wants to be closer and closer to God. Your spirit man wants to know the things of God.

We should know the things of God. God has a storehouse of knowledge He desires to impart to us. If we'll just ask questions, He'll reply. God has an answer for everything. We can know His heart.

> **My son, if you accept my words and store up my commands within you,**
>
> **Turning your ear to wisdom and applying your heart to understanding,**
>
> **And if you call out for insight and cry aloud for understanding,**
>
> **And if you look for it as for silver and search for it as for hidden treasure,**
>
> **Then you will understand the fear of the Lord and find the knowledge of God.**
>
> **For the Lord gives wisdom, and from his mouth come knowledge and understanding.**
>
> Proverbs 2:1-6 NIV

There are no *wonderings* in the realm of the spirit, there are only *knowings*. Once you begin living in the realm of the spirit, you'll no longer wonder if your prayers are going to be answered. You'll no longer wonder if you are going to survive certain situations. You'll *know* that what you have prayed about has already been answered.

That's how we should live. Enoch lived knowing God, not wondering about God. Wonderings are of the devil. Enoch never wondered because he had crossed the line over into the spirit realm and had stayed there. Never once did he turn back after he made the decision to get close to God. He decided, "I'm going to walk with God at all times. We're going to be friends." He probably said and did some things that most people didn't understand at all. When you live your life by the Spirit, people may think you're strange too.

You'll have to fight the kingdom of darkness to get there, so be prepared. The devil knows that once you have crossed over into the realm of the spirit, you will be like an atomic bomb to him. You will be a threat to him because you will be walking in the complete knowledge that everything is done NOW. You'll be able to say to the devil, "You can't do that. No, you don't! Go, in the name of Jesus!" and he will have to go because of the authority you have in Christ Jesus.

You will be so in tune with God that you will be thinking God's thoughts! At the same instant God is thinking something, you'll know what He thought, and you'll go ahead and do it, even before He asks you to. When you are living in the realm of the spirit, you know exactly what to do, when to do it, and how to get the job done quickly.

That's where God wants us to be — walking and talking with Him as a close friend — walking hand in hand with God.

God wants fellowship with us. We should have the same testimony Enoch did. The question is: What price are we willing to pay for it? We can't be friends with the world and friends with God at the same time. The price is different for every person. What is it you are holding on to? What is it that you honor and place before God? Maybe it's a soap opera at 2:00 every afternoon, a car, a home, another person, or even ice cream! If it is keeping you from being a friend of God, get rid of it!

OPERATING IN THE SPIRIT

When you walk with God as a friend, you'll be like the saints of old. When Peter and John arrived at the Gate Beautiful, they saw a lame man. Peter said to him, **Silver and gold have I none; but such as I have give I thee: In the name of Jesus Christ of Nazareth rise up and walk** (Acts 3:6). That didn't come out of Peter's natural mind. If it had, that crippled man would have remained lame. But Peter was operating by the power of the Holy Spirit.

The Amplified Bible says Peter **took hold of the man's right hand with a firm grip and raised him up** (Acts 3:7). Peter knew because of his faith in God, that the lame man was going to be healed. He didn't wait for the man to stand up on his own. Peter helped him up right away, and as he did, the man's ankle bones and feet became strong — strong enough to begin walking, and leaping, and praising God.

Peter's spirit man knew God wanted to heal this man. Our spirit man always knows God's plans. We think in the past, present, and future, but God always thinks in the NOW. We're the ones who say "wait" or "it can't be done." Our heads say that, but our spirit man agrees with God. And when our spirit man rules we walk with God in the NOW.

When your spirit rules, your mind might say, "No, don't do that," but you will follow after what your spirit says because it's the ruler. You will say and do things that will impact your world for God because you're living by His Spirit. If we would listen to the inward voice of the Holy Spirit at all times, we never would fall into problems. We would always know what needs to be done.

If it worked for Enoch and the prophets of old, it will work for you. God is no respecter of persons. What He's done for others, He will do for you. So give your all to God. Get close to Him, and you will find yourself walking with Him as a best friend. You can be God-conscious every day of your life.

Chapter 7

Living a Holy Life Before All

Be ye holy; for I am holy.

1 Peter 1:16

Living a holy life before God and others is a major key to success. *Holiness* simply means to be separated unto God. As Christians, we have been taken out of the world of sin and translated into God's world, which is holy.

For God hath not called us unto uncleanness, but unto holiness.

1 Thessalonians 4:7

Holiness is not a list of do's and don'ts as many have taught in the past. Holiness is a way of life — a lifestyle free from sin.

Asking the Lord to save you is more than just fire insurance! Many people live like the devil all week long, then go to church on Sundays thinking that will make them righteous and give them passage to heaven. But you can't live like that and expect to go to heaven. There's more to the Christian walk than getting saved and going to church on Sundays. It's not leaving your hair uncut and removing all your makeup and jewelry, either.

Holiness is living a holy life every day of the week, trusting God, living with Him, and doing what is right to the best of our ability. There's no place for willful sin in a walk of holiness before God. Yes, I believe in preaching God is a good God. Yes, He's a God of love. But there's also a judgment side to His character. He hates sin.

We can't go around saying, "Well, God is a good God — He'll forgive me," and continue to do what we know is wrong. God is not impressed when people say, "God will forgive me," when they have no thought of repenting. That's sin. Sin separates us from God. We rob ourselves of a *relationship* with God when we live a sinful lifestyle. Sin presents an obstacle in our prayer life. If we are not walking in His righteousness, how can He impart divine wisdom and knowledge to us? We must learn to repent quickly and mean what we say.

Oral Roberts once told the Oral Roberts University student body, "The most important part of any service is what happens to you on the inside. What counts is that what you have heard on the inside comes to the outside."

Ephesians 5:27 tells us that Jesus is coming for a Church without spot or wrinkle. God desires to have a glorious

Church. The spots and wrinkles are the sins of the believers. Notice I said they are the sins of believers, not sinners.

Believers have no excuse for sin of any kind in their lives. Sin blocks your relationship with God. Sin pulls you out of the realm of the Spirit. Sin stops the power of God from flowing in your life. Sin will destroy you!

When preachers in the past started sinning, they lost their power, their crowds, their money, their families, and everything else. Soon they lost their lives. They lost it all.

Sin is sin in God's eyes. There is no degree of sin in His eyes. If you lie, it's just like committing murder. If you murder, it's just like lying. There's no greater or lesser sin. Today we classify sin. We say, "Oh, that's not too bad. We shouldn't do this, but we can get away with that." According to God's Word, we can't get away with any kind of sin.

> **Blessed is the man that walketh not in the counsel of the ungodly, nor standeth in the way of sinners, nor sitteth in the seat of the scornful.**
>
> **But his delight is in the law of the Lord; and in his law doth he meditate day and night.**
>
> **And he shall be like a tree planted by the rivers of water, that bringeth forth his fruit in his season; his leaf also shall not wither; and whatsoever he doeth shall prosper.**
>
> **Psalm 1:1-3**

We're not even to associate with people who sin, lest we fall into sin ourselves. Do not bow down to peer pressure. Let your delight be in the Word of God, not in the sinful behavior of those around you. Be strong like the tree planted by the rivers of water.

> Blessed are the undefiled in the way, who walk in the law of the Lord.
>
> Blessed are they that keep his testimonies, and that seek him with the whole heart.
>
> Psalm 119:1-2

> Know ye not that the unrighteous shall not inherit the kingdom of God? Be not deceived: neither fornicators, nor idolaters, nor adulterers, nor effeminate, nor abusers of themselves with mankind,
>
> Nor thieves, nor covetous, nor drunkards, nor revilers, nor extortioners, shall inherit the kingdom of God.
>
> And such were some of you: but ye are washed, but ye are sanctified, but ye are justified in the name of the Lord Jesus, and by the Spirit of our God.
>
> 1 Corinthians 6:9-11

God has called us to holiness.

MENTAL SINS

Most believers have their outward man pretty well organized. Whatever is happening on the inside can pretty much be kept well hidden — for a time. We act right, talk right, look right, and do most things according to what is expected of us, and people don't always see our true selves. But there is one area that has caused many problems for believers today — mental sins.

Just because we say the right things and do the right things, it doesn't mean all is right with us. How is our inside? How is our mind? Is it stayed on the things of God, or does it wander off into the things of the world? The wandering mind usually ends up sinning greatly, because that is where sin is birthed — in the mind as a thought. One reason Christians have trouble keeping their mind on the Lord is because they have a lot of idle time on their hands. Idle time is the devil's time, and a mind that is not kept focused on the things of God causes more mental sins than anything else.

Let not sin therefore reign in your mortal body, that ye should obey it in the lusts thereof.

Neither yield ye your members as instruments of unrighteousness unto sin: but yield yourselves unto God, as those that are alive from the dead, and your members as instruments of righteousness unto God.

For sin shall not have dominion over you: for ye are not under the law, but under grace.

What then? shall we sin, because we are not under the law, but under grace? God forbid.

Know ye not, that to whom ye yield yourselves servants to obey, his servants ye are to whom ye obey; whether of sin unto death, or of obedience unto righteousness?

Romans 6:12-16

There are two key words in the above scripture — LET NOT!
Let not has nothing to do with the power of God or the devil. It
has everything to do with an individual's will. When you sin,
you are making the decision to sin. Some people say, "The devil
made me do it." Others say, "I just couldn't help myself. That's
just the way I am." But according to the Word of God, that is
simply not true.

People use all kinds of excuses for sin, but God's Word says
to us: LET NOT. That means it is our personal will that decides
to sin or not to sin. We are a servant to whatever we yield ourselves to. It is our choice, and ours alone.

Ye have heard that it was said by them of old time,
Thou shall not commit adultery:

But I say unto you, That whosoever looketh on a
woman to lust after her hath committed adultery with
her already in his heart.

Matthew 5:27-28

Jesus told them, "If you looked with lust on a woman, you
have sinned." It was no different than committing the act of
adultery itself.

The mind must be tamed. The mind must be brought under
control. If your mind wanders, thinks what it wants to think,
and imagines what it wants to imagine, sin is bound to be the
end result.

Finally, brethren, whatsoever things are true, whatsoever things are honest, whatsoever things are just,

whatsoever things are pure, whatsoever things are lovely, whatsoever things are of good report; if there be any virtue, and if there be any praise, think on these things.

Philippians 4:8

We must *discipline* our mind to think only on those things that are true, honest, just, pure, lovely, and of good report. We shouldn't allow ourselves to think on anything else. If you say, "But I can't do that," you're not disciplined yet. If you can't tell your mind what to think and keep it under control, you need to spend more time in the Word, filling it with what God says about things and what He thinks about things.

That ye put off concerning the former conversation the old man, which is corrupt according to the deceitful lusts;

And be renewed in the spirit of your mind;

And that ye put on the new man, which after God is created in righteousness and true holiness.

Ephesians 4:22-24

A preacher who stands in the pulpit and lusts after a woman in his congregation is sinning. You would be surprised at how many preachers do that. When they stand before God on Judgment Day, He's going to ask them, "Why did you do that?" There won't be any room for excuses then. The preacher won't be able to say, "I was in the flesh," or "I didn't know better." God gave us the Word so we would know better. He gave us power and authority so we would NOT sin. It is up to us to stop sinning.

Do you yield your mind, body, and spirit to God, or do you yield yourself to the temptations of sin? When you accept the temptations of sin and do them, you are working for Satan's kingdom, not God's.

If you sin, it's your fault. You can't blame it on anyone else, including God or the devil, and you can't blame it on your circumstances. As a believer, you should rule circumstances. You should be able to overcome every obstacle you face. You have been given all authority and power from heaven to rule circumstances and not let them control you. You don't have to yield yourself to pressures.

The only thing the devil can feed you is the *temptation* to sin. He puts the temptation to sin before you, but he doesn't commit the sin for you nor does he *make* you sin. You either accept the temptation and do it, or you refuse to do it.

Submit yourselves therefore to God. Resist the devil, and he will flee from you.

James 4:7

Whenever a temptation to sin is placed before you, there is a decision you must make: *Am I going to yield myself to this sin, or am I going to yield myself to God?*

You also can't use the excuse that sin happened because of your flesh. You should rule your own flesh. If you want the power of God in your life, you must quit sinning and start doing what is right. Tryers never will make it; doers will. You don't *try to* sin or *try not* to sin. You either sin or you don't sin! When temptation comes, resist the devil and refuse to receive that temptation.

Sin must cease in the lives of believers and ministers; otherwise, the Church will be without power. When you sin, you lose power, and you lose contact with God's throne room. God will not pour His glory into a vessel that has sin in it. Sin and glory cannot mix. It causes an explosion called judgment.

That's what happened to Ananias and Sapphira in the fifth chapter of Acts. They lied and died! They didn't die just because the apostles were standing there. They died because they walked into the glory, power, and presence of God with sin in their lives. They disobeyed God. They were not operating in the wisdom of the Lord and had become foolish in their actions. (See Acts 5:1-11.)

If they had been in right relationship with God, that never would have happened. Sin in the presence of God caused a reaction. The apostles had nothing to do with it. God had nothing to do with it. They killed themselves. They committed suicide spiritually.

If you walk inside a place where God's power is manifested and there is sin in your life, you better be scared because it is possible God's judgment will fall. I believe it's going to start happening more and more in the days to come.

A LIFESTYLE OF HOLINESS OR SIN

The fear of the Lord is the beginning of knowlege: but fools despise wisdom and instruction.

Proverbs 1:7

I find it difficult to understand why some Christians live in sin. It doesn't make any sense at all! People who live holy lives before God don't understand sin because they live with the fear of God in their lives.

We need the reverential fear of God in our lives. If we had it like the old-timers had it in the past, we would be less apt to sin. Those old-timers reverenced God. They wouldn't have dreamed of sinning in God's presence — ever. They feared the awesomeness of God and His mighty power. There's nothing wrong with that! It causes us to live right when we reverence and fear God.

Back in the old days, God's name was highly reverenced. Today, we let people use God's name in vain and we don't say a word about it. We don't revolt when they use it on television. Some sit in theaters and smile and laugh along with everyone else when God's name is used in vain.

That's the God who lives on the inside of you! That's the God who created you! That's the God who has blessed you and helps you every day. Yet we sit back and laugh! That's not right.

Love and respect for God will cause you to stand up and say, "Stop it! That's my God. Don't use that kind of language around me." Some say the Gospel needs no defense, but I still like to stand up for my Friend. The fear of God will cause you to stand up for what is right.

We need to reverence God like some of the old-timers did. We need to shake and quake when we do something wrong! Sin has no place in a believer's life. Jonathan Edwards preached a powerful sermon called, "Sinners in the Hands of an Angry God," which dealt with holiness and sin. Every time he preached that sermon the power of God fell.

Edwards couldn't see too well so he wore thick-rimmed glasses and would stick his sermon notes right up in front of his face in order to read them. He couldn't see his audience very clearly, but when he began to preach from those notes, people would begin to quake, shake, and cry out to God in repentance. That is the power of God. We need power like that today. I believe if there were a few more preachers in our churches today like there were in the old days, we would be a lot better off. Yes, God is a loving, forgiving, merciful God, but that doesn't mean we can go on sinning. We can't use God's love as a license to sin.

Having therefore these promises, dearly beloved, let us cleanse ourselves from all filthiness of the flesh and spirit, perfecting holiness in the fear of God.

2 Corinthians 7:1

God's love doesn't mean we can go out and sin tonight, then act real nice tomorrow morning as if nothing happened.

I was with some ministers one time who suggested that we go see a movie. Now, I like to see a good movie every once in awhile, but the trouble is, there aren't many good ones around anymore! All the cussing and violence bother me greatly. I can't stand it, and I've been known to get up from a movie and walk out.

These ministers said, "Let's go see such-and-such movie. God will forgive us tomorrow." They all laughed about it, but I almost fell out of my chair. I thought, *No wonder there's no power in their churches. No wonder they all look at me like I'm strange.*

I spoke up, "I'm sorry, but I can't go with you. You go if you want, but I'm not going with you. I've got standards I stick to, and I'm not going to bend them by seeing that movie."

They looked at me smugly with an *oh, you're so spiritual* look. If you call that superspiritual, I don't care. Going against convictions the Holy Spirit has placed within me is sin! It would have been sin for me to shrug aside my beliefs to go along with the crowd. You can't do such things and expect to see God's power in your life. You can't knowingly sin and ask for forgiveness morning after morning.

As easy as it is to sin, it's just as easy to do what is right! All you have to do is decide which road you are going to travel on — the road of sin or the road of righteousness. It's that easy.

Some people look at other people smoking and drinking and say, "They're sinning. How can they ever be saved? How can they ever be filled with the Holy Spirit?" Then they themselves go out and cuss, commit adultery in their minds, and think all kinds of awful, hateful things. That's just as much sin.

I heard a preacher say, "If you're going to sin, go ahead and sin BIG." Sin is sin.

If you don't quit sinning and start doing what God says, you're not going to get very far. It wasn't God's will for the children of Israel to go into captivity. They brought it on their own heads because of their disobedience to God, which is sin. They played games with God. They said they would follow the laws of God, but they didn't. They even began to worship false gods. Games and cheap talk don't impress God! God wants to see action. God wants our obedience.

> **Behold, ye have sinned against the Lord: and be sure your sin will find you out.**
>
> **Numbers 32:23**

There will always be consequences to sin. If you go out and sin and still carry the name of God, your sin will be found out. There will be a reproach on your life and upon the body of Christ. The spiritual consequence of separation from God is bad enough, but you can find examples throughout the Bible of men and women who suffered serious consequences in the natural because of their sinful ways. (See Genesis 6,7; 1 Samuel 2:27-36; 2 Samuel 12:1-19.)

When you stand before Almighty God, He may ask you, "Why did you do that?" If you reply, "I just wanted to try it out," He'll say, "Not good enough!" He'll say, "I told you not to." You'll reply, "I was in the flesh!" God will say, "Who cares? Didn't I give you the power and the authority to overcome the flesh? Didn't I give you an individual will?" We will answer on our own.

> Let not sin therefore reign in your mortal body, that ye should obey it in the lusts thereof.
>
> **Romans 6:12**

SOWING SEEDS

> No good tree bears bad fruit, nor does a bad tree bear good fruit.
> Each tree is recognized by its own fruit. People do not pick figs from thornbushes, or grapes from briers.
> The good man brings good things out of the good stored up in his heart, and the evil man brings evil things out of the evil stored up in his heart. For out of the overflow of his heart his mouth speaks.
>
> **Luke 6:43-45** NIV

When you sin, you sow a seed. You cannot uproot the seeds that have been sown, and you will reap whatever that seed produces. When a seed is sown, it produces fruit. When you sow a seed of willful sin, that seed is going to grow. Believe me, the devil will make sure the seed is fed and watered! It will come forth and bring evil fruit. You sowed and you will reap. God does not cause the seed to grow and produce fruit — you do. Even good seed has to be watered. You have to keep it watered and fed with the Word.

> **Be not deceived; God is not mocked: for whatsoever a man soweth, that shall he also reap.**
>
> **For he that soweth to his flesh shall of the flesh reap corruption; but he that soweth to the Spirit shall of the Spirit reap life everlasting.**
>
> **And let us not be weary in well doing: for in due season we shall reap, if we faint not.**
>
> **Galatians 6:7-9**

When you sow a seed, you will reap a harvest — no matter whether that seed is a good seed or an evil seed. I want a harvest of good in my life, so I have to sow good seeds.

One reason Christians have problems is because they have sown the seed of strife in their homes. They complain about the discord in their home, but the truth is, they have brought it on their own heads.

People say, "But we live in this world — we can't help it." Yes, you can! God gave us His Word for guidance and direction. He told us what was what. It's up to us to read it and obey it. It's not that hard to obey the laws of our glorious God. Remember, as easy as it is to sin, it's just as easy to do right!

What about the sin of ignorance? People ask me this all the time. Does God allow sin due to ignorance, or is He more lenient with those who just don't know any better? Some people would say yes, but I don't agree. We don't have any excuse for ignorance. God has given us all the knowledge we need in His Word. People perish for lack of knowledge. (See Proverbs 29:18.) Ignorance is no excuse.

When Jesus went to heaven He sent the Holy Spirit, our Great Teacher, to guide us into ALL truth.

> Howbeit when he, the Spirit of truth, is come, he will guide you into all truth: for he shall not speak of himself; but whatsoever he shall hear, that shall he speak: and he will shew you things to come.
>
> John 16:13

If we are led by the Spirit of God, we are the children of God. The Spirit of God does not know defeat, failure, or sin. He can only guide an individual into all TRUTH, VICTORY, and SUCCESS in life. The sin of ignorance does not exist for us because the Spirit of God guides us on the right pathway. There is no excuse for us to continue in sin.

> If ye then be risen with Christ, seek those things which are above, where Christ sitteth on the right hand of God.
>
> Set your affection on things above, not on things on the earth.
>
> Colossians 3:1-2

For God hath not called us unto uncleanness, but unto holiness.

1 Thessalonians 4:7

CHAPTER 8

HINDRANCES TO SUCCESS

There are three areas I am going to cover in this chapter — marriage, money, and spiritual pride. There have been more failures in these three areas in Christians' lives than anything else I know of.

GOD'S MARRIAGE PLANS FOR YOU

A successful marriage is a blessing of God. God created the institution of marriage. He compares marriage with Christ and the Church. Many great and glorious things can be said about marriage, but a bad marriage can be disastrous for believers and ministers.

When thinking about marriage, many people neglect seeking God's wisdom and direction. They never get His answer about whom they should marry because they never ask! Many ministries and families have been destroyed because they married the wrong person. They didn't seek God about their marriage.

Kathryn Kuhlman's marriage almost destroyed her and her ministry. During the Depression in the 1930s, she held revival meetings in Denver, Colorado. Thousands were saved in those meetings, and the people begged her to stay and start a church. Denver Revival Tabernacle was built and she stayed there for several years.

In 1938, against everyone's advice, she married a man who had divorced his wife and left two children to marry her. They sold Denver Revival Tabernacle, traveled north to Iowa, and not much was heard of Kathryn again until 1946.

Those eight years were horrible years for Miss Kuhlman. She suffered tremendously. Then in 1944, she left her husband and went East. In spite of her mistakes and weaknesses, the mighty compassion, mercy, and grace of the Lord flowed through her again. She began holding services in Pennsylvania and started a radio program. From that day forward, her ministry began to take off again, but she could have saved herself many years of sorrow by simply asking God about the man she was or was not to marry.

Others have had similar stories. Aimee Semple McPherson and John Alexander Dowie also had marriage difficulties that affected them and their ministries.

Today, the divorce rate among Christians is astronomical. That is not God's way. If He brings people together, they should stay together. If He didn't bring them together, they should never have gotten married in the first place.

In counseling young people, I tell them not to date everyone who comes along. I don't care how nice looking the girl may be or how popular she is. Before you ever ask someone for a date, you should get down on your knees and ask God, "Is it okay to ask this person out?" If He says, "No, don't do it," there are reasons He doesn't want you going out with that person, and for your own safety, you better heed the word of the Lord!

There have been too many mistakes made on dates that God never sanctioned in the first place. Dating the wrong person can lead you into marrying the wrong person because every date is a potential marriage. The first date is the first step toward marriage.

Marriages are not 50/50 propositions — they are 100/100 propositions. You cannot give 50 percent and expect your mate to give 50 percent. If you do that, when the trials and hardships come and one of you pulls back just 5 percent, that opens the door for the devil to come in. But when you are giving 100 percent and your mate is giving 100 percent, you have a wall surrounding you that will keep the devil out of your marriage.

If you can't go 100 percent with someone, don't marry that person. Too many people who have walked the aisle and said, "I do," wished later that they hadn't. That should never happen in a marriage, and it won't if God is in it.

One thing that destroys marriages quicker than anything else is mistaken priorities. After the Lord, your mate should be the most important thing in your life. Many ministers forget this. They wind up putting the ministry before their mates. People in the secular world often put their jobs before their families, and this is also wrong.

The ministry can wait. Your job can wait. But the family can't wait. The ministry or the job doesn't depend on you anyway, it depends on God. Ministers who have problems with their families should straighten those problems out before they continue ministering. Your home life has to flow with the unity of God in order for you to have power in your life.

I know of a minister who married and then went on the mission field. He took an entire South American country for God. The entire government staff sat on the stage while he preached the Gospel. The president was born again under this man's ministry. He was used mightily of God. But then he left the mission field and came home because his wife kept saying, "Come home, come home." She didn't add to that man, she pulled from him.

We need wives and husbands who will support us, not pull against us. This man died in 1976 a divorced alcoholic! Why? He married the wrong person, and it ruined him.

And every man that striveth for the mastery is temperate in all things.

1 Corinthians 9:25

God has put natural desires into every man and woman. We've got a spirit, a soul, and a body. Each of these three areas has needs and they must be met. They are natural, God-given desires that must be met and if they aren't met in the right way, trouble arises.

Many times an individual will go all out meeting the needs of one area while neglecting the other areas of their life. The day will come when those desires that have been sacrificed must be fulfilled. People can choose to fulfill those desires God's way, or they can choose to let the world meet their desires. If they go into the world to fullfill their needs rather than going to God, they rarely return.

MAINTAINING A PROPER BALANCE

These God-given desires must be met. There are spiritual desires such as praying, fellowshipping with the brethren, and studying the Word of God. Then there are natural desires within an individual that must be met as well. An individual must have interaction with other people, and they must know what it is to relax. If these natural desires aren't met correctly, the day will come when the desires and needs will surface. Those needs will become so great, they will cause rapid changes in one's life.

Let me give you an example. There was a very popular child evangelist a few years back who is not much older than I am. When he was very young, all he did was preach. He was a dynamic preacher, and thousands of people came to his meetings. There was an anointing on his life, and he was used mightily of God.

The only problem was that his parents never let him be a normal little boy. I have talked to people who traveled with this boy and they said he would always ask his parents, "Mom, Dad, can we go home now? I want to be with my friends." They always said, "No, we've got to go preach. We've got another meeting to go to."

The day finally came when that young man was old enough to make some of his own decisions and he totally quit the ministry. He turned his back on God and everything associated with the ministry. He said, "I'm never going back to the ministry. I'm going to live!"

He wanted to live! That's a sad story. It should never have ended like that. If his parents had used godly wisdom, they would have taken some time off once in a while to let that young boy rest, spend time with his friends, and have a normal childhood. His spiritual life was totally out of balance with everything else.

We need to re-evaluate some of the things we're doing. People who stay locked up all the time in prayer closets and never come out usually end up having some very weird doctrine. I know what it means to stay in the prayer closet and pray. Most of us need to do it more often. But God didn't say to stay in there for eternity! We need to stay in our prayer closets until God moves. I'm firmly convinced we need to spend a lot of time in our prayer closets, but let's not get flaky about it. Flaky believers bring a reproach to the Gospel.

We must be very careful in our spiritual walk to not get weird, out of balance, and do flaky things. Let's not get off on strange tangents. Let's not be spotted and wrinkled!

FINANCIAL WOES

Money is a big problem in many people's lives today — in their marriages and in their ministries. Money has become many people's god. They look to money to solve all their problems.

But seek ye first the kingdom of God, and his right-eousness; and all these things shall be added unto you.

Take therefore no thought for the morrow: for the morrow shall take thought for the things of itself.

Matthew 6:33-34

If you are obedient to God and His Word, you will have no problem with finances! God will meet all your needs if you seek His kingdom first.

God expects ministers and believers to be people of integrity with their finances. God does not believe in gimmicks.

Yet have I not seen the righteous forsaken, nor his seed begging bread.

Psalm 37:25

God's plan is not for believers to be beggars. Believers who have trouble managing their finances need God's wisdom. There are many Christian financial counselors who can help people, through God's Word, get their finances on track.

Before I ever went into the ministry, God told me to start paying tithes and to give an offering toward my ministry in the future. I wasn't doing much back then, just mowing lawns and watching a group of children for a family I knew. God told me to give five dollars to three different ministries. Every week I faithfully sent off my fifteen dollars — five dollars to Oral Roberts, five dollars to Kenneth Hagin, and five dollars to Jerry B. Walker. I was sowing seeds I would reap a harvest from in the future.

When I first started out in ministry, I would look at my empty calendar. No one knew who I was. No one cared who I was! But I knew God had called me to preach. So, I would look at my calendar and tell it to fill up with good church engagements. I would say, "One day calendar, you're not going to be big enough to hold all the speaking engagements God has for me."

I have never had any problems getting meetings. I have been booked up since I started. Ministers should never have any problem with finances or with finding places to minister if they start where they are at and are faithful. God will bless your faithfulness and diligence. He will equip you with all the finances you need.

SPIRITUAL PRIDE

Spiritual pride says, "Look what happens when I pray!" People with spiritual pride are always drawing attention to themselves. Spiritual pride is a constant threat to successful believers and ministers and it is a constant battle to run from. Yes, you have to run from it. The second it comes knocking at your door, tell it to get lost.

You have to fight spiritual pride every day of your life. It's not something you can get rid of once and for all. It will often pop up its ugly head when you least suspect it. But you don't have to give in to it. If you do, you're dead. Spiritual pride will destroy you.

My grandmother once lived with Oral Roberts' mother. Momma Roberts was a little woman and Oral was very tall, but she would grab Oral's ear, pull him down, and say, "Oral, stay small in your own eyes. I don't care how great people think you are or say you are. The day you start thinking that you're great is the day you'll fall. Stay away from that pride. Stay small in your own eyes. Know that God has made you."

Every believer needs to remember that. God has made us who we are. We need to know how to receive compliments graciously without letting them puff us up.

The Word of God says that knowledge puffs up. There are some people who actually lust after knowledge. They run from meeting to meeting seeking after some new revelation. They're not being doers of the Word with what they already have. They just want to accumulate more knowledge. They become dry and stagnant because they aren't doers of the Word, but merely hearers of it. We are to take the Word that is in us and put it to action, not let it sit in our mind and become mush.

The original sin in the Garden of Eden came about because Eve lusted after knowledge. She chose to eat of the tree of the knowledge of good and evil. Her lust for knowledge was her downfall.

Drug addicts lust after more and more drugs. They may start off just smoking marijuana, but before you know it, they want something stronger. As they go along, it takes more to satisfy them. Their senses become dull and they crave more and more. Nothing really satisfies them after awhile and they become totally preoccupied with feeding their lust.

I have seen this with some very materialistic people as well. They want more and more *things*. They buy and buy, but eventually what they are buying doesn't mean anything to them any longer. They just get caught up in lusting after things.

It's the same with many Christians and the desire for more and more knowledge. There is nothing wrong with wanting to know more about God. The more we know God's character, the more we can become like Him. Spiritual pride enters the picture when that little bit of knowledge becomes greater than anything else in your life. You are so proud of the fact that you know what the Word has to say about certain things, and you want everyone else to know how proud you are of yourself! The cure for spiritual pride is humility.

God resisteth the proud, but giveth grace unto the humble.

Humble yourselves in the sight of the Lord, and he shall lift you up.

James 4:6,10

Humble yourselves therefore under the mighty hand of God, that he may exalt you in due time.

1 Peter 5:6

STAYING OPEN TO THE MOVES OF GOD

Spiritual pride causes people to get stuck in ruts! When God wants to do a new work in us, we are not open to it because we think we already know it all. We must be able to change when God says change. He doesn't want us to stay put where we're at and form little groups that never change. God hasn't called us to be little groupies — He has called us to go out and change the world for Him.

People often say to me, "God's not moving like He used to." They don't know what to expect next, or they're not seeing God move in a way they expect, so they're afraid He's not moving at all. God's got it all in control. When God is making changes and doing something new, just go along with Him. He knows what is around the corner. Don't put God in a box or limit what you think He can do.

Some cults are formed by people who aren't open to change. They get stuck on one idea or one way of doing things. They started out all right, but when God began to move in a new direction, they dug their heels in and stayed put. They began doing things according to their own wisdom rather than God's and ended up doing some very weird things and believing some very wrong doctrine.

If we move on with God, He'll stay with us. The body of Christ has seen many changes over the years. Some people haven't liked the changes. Others are going on with God. But it's not up to us whether we do or don't like something God wants to do. He has a divine plan for our lives and we should be willing to do whatever it takes to have that plan fulfilled in our lives.

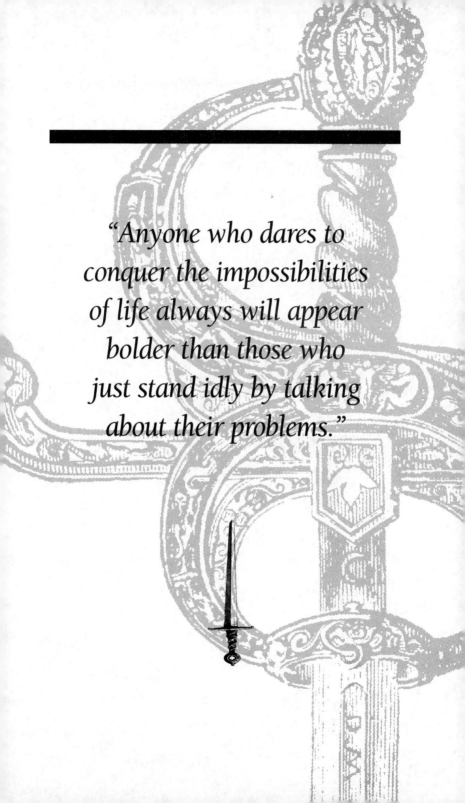

"Anyone who dares to conquer the impossibilities of life always will appear bolder than those who just stand idly by talking about their problems."

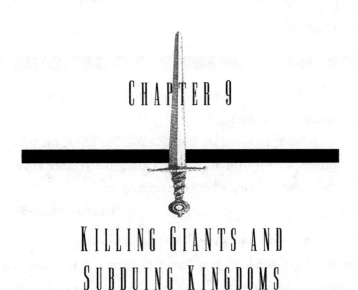

CHAPTER 9

KILLING GIANTS AND SUBDUING KINGDOMS

God wants us to experience the heights of His glory. He wants to take us into His glory world. We can walk in the kind of success He created us to walk in. By applying the principles discussed in the book to our lives and ministries, we can experience God's glory world.

The characteristics of the great men and women of God throughout history are similar to the great heroes of faith told of in the Bible. They could be listed in the Great Hall of Faith because they fulfilled what Hebrews 11 talks about.

> Who through faith subdued kingdoms, wrought righteousness, obtained promises, stopped the mouths of lions,
>
> Quenched the violence of fire, escaped the edge of the sword, out of weakness were made

strong, waxed valiant in fight, turned to flight the armies of the aliens.

Women received their dead raised to life again: and others were tortured, not accepting deliverance; that they might obtain a better resurrection.

Hebrews 11:33-35

Through their faith in God, successful Christians throughout history have subdued kingdoms! Faith is the key. You can't subdue kingdoms without faith. And you can't subdue anything of significance if you haven't first subdued the little things in your life. That is why the life of David is so encouraging. David is one of the great men of faith spoken of in Hebrews 11:32. God used David mightily, but David started out just a simple little shepherd boy. How could he ever amount to anything?

One of the best known stories of David's life was when he killed Goliath. (See 1 Samuel 17:4-51.) David killed the giant, Goliath, but he never would have been able to if he hadn't first subdued the lion and the bear in his life. He had experience and training behind him before he ever tackled the giant. Many Christians and preachers today are trying to kill giants and subdue kingdoms before they have learned to first subdue the lions and the bears in their own lives.

Goliath mocked God and His army. When David arrived, he looked at the giant making all the noise, he saw all the people cowering in fear, and he boldly said, "Why doesn't someone take care of that obnoxious man? Why are you letting him stand there mocking us like that?"

Eliab, David's oldest brother, didn't much care for David's comments. Who in the world did David think he was anyway, walking into their camp and questioning them about how they were or were not handling the giant? He was just a young shepherd boy. What did he know anyway? Plenty! He knew his God.

Anyone who dares to conquer the impossibilities of life will always appear bolder than those who just stand idly by talking about their problems. They will always accuse you of bragging, but you don't have to say a word to justify yourself. David didn't. He just took care of the problem. He backed up his words with action. He proved that the giant could be defeated.

Everyone else in the camp was petrified of the Philistine, but not David. He boldly stated, "I'll take care of him then, if no one else will." He was the only one with the backbone to volunteer. In an effort to help, Saul tried to put his armor on David, but it didn't fit. David took it right off.

People still do that today. Just as Saul tried to get David to use his armor and do it his way, people today stand around with their "armors." They are always ready to give you their "armor" of advice about the way you should or should not do things. They will say, "Do it this way. I did it this way and it worked for me. It will work for you too."

Don't listen to them! Do it God's way like David did. When Saul questioned David's youth, training, and experience, David again boldly replied:

> Thy servant kept his father's sheep, and there came a lion, and a bear, and they took a lamb out of the flock:
>
> And I went out after him and smote him, and delivered it out of his mouth: and when he arose against me, I caught him by his beard, and smote him, and slew him.
>
> Thy servant slew both the lion and the bear: and this uncircumcised Philistine shall be as one of them, seeing he hath defied the armies of the living God.
>
> 1 Samuel 17:34-36

David knew what it was like to flow in God's power and anointing. He had already fought battles with lions and bears. He didn't run from those battles — he faced them and won. He had learned to flow and yield to the power and anointing of God in his life.

The lions and the bears are the problems that beset you as you are growing up in your spiritual walk and ministry. We will never be successful Christians or ministers if we ignore the lions and bears in our lives. We must conquer them first before we try to conquer giants and subdue kingdoms. Be determined to fight those lions and bears, and be determined to win.

My grandmother built within me the determination to do battle. Through prayer, a backbone of steel was built in me.

Some Christians and ministers have backbones like jellyfish — no backbone at all! Jellyfish don't have backbones. They float around doing nothing and the current carries them every which way.

Believers and ministers need backbones of steel. With a backbone like that, you'll decide to stick to what you believe, no matter what happens. If the whole world stands against you, you'll still be standing there fighting. That's what we need in the body of Christ today.

That backbone comes from only one thing — knowing God. You can't get it from knowing other individuals. You can't get it by playing games with God or by trying out different formulas for overnight success. I don't care who lays hands on you, who prays for you, or who blows on you — a backbone of steel comes from knowing your God.

When I say knowing God, I mean *knowing* Him. I don't mean knowing *about* Him by listening to other people or by reading books. The only way to know God personally and intimately is to spend time with Him — pray, read His Word, and praise and worship Him. As you get to know God and what He likes and dislikes, you will conquer bears, lions, and eventually giants. You will subdue kingdoms!

I have had to subdue a lot of lions and bears. I remember the first time a drunkard was set free in one of my meetings. The Spirit of God was demonstrating His power that night through signs and wonders, and this drunk man got in line to be prayed for.

When I looked at him, tears began to stream down his face. He said to me, "I'm old enough to remember when they lined up people just like this in the big tents. I was in one of those prayer lines one night when Brother Allen got hold of me and set me free. But I'm back in the gutter again. I need help."

Then he said something I'll never forget as long as I live, "Isn't there anyone who walks in the power like they did back then? Isn't there anyone who can set me free? Isn't there anyone left like that today?"

God delivered that man that night. Hallelujah! But later in the evening as I was thinking about what that man said, it bothered me. I began to wonder, *Why aren't there more ministers like that today?* Now that man can't blame anyone else except himself for falling back into sin. You can have someone lay hands on you, pray for you, and help set you free, but it is up to you to stay free. Nevertheless, his question concerning mighty men and women of God with power still made me think a minute.

Where are all the John Wesleys who would get up at four in the morning to pray and seek the face of God?

Where are the George Whitefields who could preach circles around all the other preachers? There was so much power in Whitefield's words that when he preached, thousands were slain by God's power.

Where are all the Smith Wigglesworths who raised people from the dead?

Where are all the Charles Finneys of today? When Finney came riding through town in his horse and buggy, the whole town would fall under the conviction of the Holy Spirit and get saved! That was God's power.

Where are all the Maria Woodworth-Etters who would stand up and say, "So be it," and it happened? When people denounced God in Etter's meetings, saying God was dead and she was a fake, Etter would point at them and say, "So be your judgment." And their mouths would be shut up tight! They couldn't even open them! Some people even died! That was God's power.

We can walk in God's power like that today! His power hasn't died off. It's still available to us today just like it has always been. All we have to do is receive it.

That divine power comes from a divine walk in the Spirit of God, and we can have that power manifested in our lives. The world needs God's power. It is up to us to walk in God's power and show the world He is real, He loves them, and He wants everyone to walk in His success realm. Like the apostle Paul, we must be able to say:

> **My message and my preaching were not with wise and persuasive words, but with a demonstration of the Spirit's power,**

So that your faith might not rest on men's wisdom, but on God's power.

1 Corinthians 2:4-5 NIV

Let us show forth the power of God, so it will also be said of us:

Who through faith subdued kingdoms, wrought righteousness, obtained promises, stopped the mouths of lions.

Hebrews 11:33

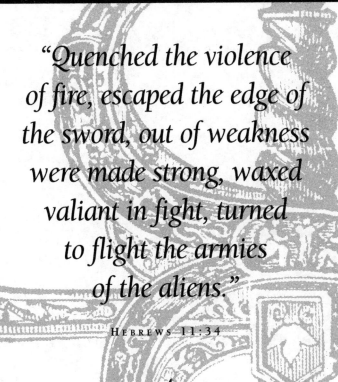

*"Quenched the violence
of fire, escaped the edge of
the sword, out of weakness
were made strong, waxed
valiant in fight, turned
to flight the armies
of the aliens."*

Hebrews 11:34

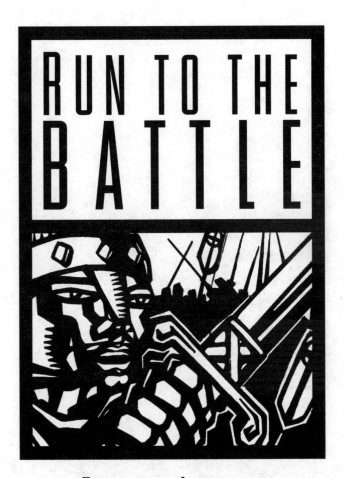

RUN TO THE BATTLE

ROBERTS LIARDON

CONTENTS

FOREWORD

by
Karl Strader
The Carpenter's Home Church
Lakeland, Florida

Roberts Liardon is a hard-hitting young man who preaches with the maturity of a well-seasoned veteran. This book is written just like Roberts preaches. Refreshing. Simple. To the point. Anointed.

The Church, the body of Christ, is in trouble. If the members will read this book, especially leaders in the Church, and respond, we can get well. This bold young man has sanctified brass that is needed to cut away the sham and the pretense of the average.

In the coming years, the Church is going to see warfare at its highest pitch. The fainthearted won't stand a chance. Whether young like Liardon, or old like me, we must be bold, aggressive, and fervent.

This book says, "Let the weak say, I am strong!" I dare you to read it through carefully and with an open heart. You'll never be the same.

INTRODUCTION

We are in a very interesting time — the end of the second millennium and the dawn of the third — since Jesus was born in Bethlehem of Judaea in the days of Caesar Augustus. We have seen major prophecies concerning His second coming fulfilled within our century.

We are getting ready to see some powerful demonstrations of the Holy Spirit, and some of them are going to challenge a lot of people. Many things people want God to do will not be granted for a time. He is going to do a great deal more cleaning before He starts granting some of the things we want to see. For example, there is going to be an acceleration of time, and it must become a friend to us rather than an enemy. The only place you can become a friend of time is in the realm of the spirit; otherwise, time is your enemy. Time is a controlling factor the flesh does not like. And we are going to see more clearly what the apostolic and the prophetic flow is for the Church.

In the 1980s, the Church began to hear about a new move of God — the former rain and the latter rain. We heard about a wind of the Spirit that would bring great signs and wonders, and we got excited about God doing a powerful revival in the earth. Then everything calmed down and got real quiet. We quit singing latter rain songs because we thought the rain had come and gone. The excitement just faded away.

But I was not satisfied in my spirit. I got on my knees and said, "God, if the latter rain came, why couldn't we tell the difference? If it came, where is all the power that was prophesied? Where are the visions and dreams? Where are the trances like the ones the Bible talks about? (See Acts 10:10; 22:17.) Why aren't our hands flowing with miracle-working power? What is going on, God?"

Years earlier, God told me to study the great men and women of the past, to find out what made them great, what made them rise, and what made them fall if they fell. In studying them, I saw that what destroyed many of them was not a lack of knowledge of the Word, nor a lack of love for God, nor a lack of a desire to help people. In many cases, personal problems caused by demonic influence caused them to fall. Those demons would lie dormant until these leaders were at their height of popularity, then move in and pull them down.

Why are miracles and power so conspicuously absent from many of our churches today? It is because few people are willing to pay the price to get to the place in God where they get beyond the devil's strongholds. Signs and wonders should be following us because the Word says so. God has not changed and will not change, so obviously we are the ones who are going to have to change if we want to be a part of the revival.

We want to get out there and work *for* God without going very deep *in* God, but He is going to require that we go deep. He has rearranged a lot of schedules. He has rearranged a lot of desires. He has rearranged a lot of what people think God has told them when He has not spoken it at all. A lot of soulish planning must be stopped and destroyed for the Church to be in prime position for this next revival.

There will be more visitations and greater prophetic utterances — scripturally characteristic of the last days. Visions belong to the young and dreams belong to the old, according to the prophet Joel. God always "telegraphs" what He is going to do with forewarnings. He tells his prophets what He is going to do. I believe He is going to forewarn us of our homegoing with visions or visits by certain people to heaven or hell.

Behold, the former things are come to pass, and new things do I declare: before they spring forth I tell you of them.

Isaiah 42:9

God is telling us before these things come forth in full measure. He is telling us of them through revelation and through demonstrations that are the firstfruits of the revival.

Yes, God is doing something new and we must be ready for it. As soon as we are ready, we have to jump into it because it is already moving. It is not coming at some vague time in the future. It is here now.

God also is beginning to unveil the leadership of the revival that has come into the earth. We are going to see new leaders rise up, and many of them are going to be young in physical age but not in spiritual maturity. Young people have a divine destiny in this hour, and it is not to run the normal course of life. There is a greater call.

Sometimes I look at the few new leaders who have been brought out, and I think, *Lord, who else are You going to put into position?*

I looked at someone and thought, *Well, they might work over there,* and the Lord said, "There is a whole new group you do not even know about."

I just want to meet them!

We have seen the hour of the teacher. I don't believe the teaching office will be the dominant anointing in the future. I am not saying there are no more teachers — teachers will never disappear. However, *there will come preachers blasting into the revival.* They will cause a great disturbance in the realm of the spirit, and they will reap a harvest that we have been foreseeing and prophesying about.

This move of God is different from most of the past moves. Man did not have to work very hard to receive them. The

Spirit did most of it. Man did not have to strive very hard to be part of the Voice of Healing move, or the Word of Faith move, or the Charismatic move. There was intercession, conflict, trials, and persecution involved, particularly for the leaders, but most of the average believers needed very little effort to be part of those moves.

However, this last move involves an individual effort because holiness is such a big part of it. You cannot just slide into this move. This one takes individual commitment. This one demands a change in the spirit, soul, and body.

Jesus said, **For unto whomsoever much is given, of him shall be much required** (Luke 12:48). No other generation has been given as much Scripture and as much revelation as this one. God is requiring more of us. He will not allow us to quote scriptures like a machine gun and then go out and commit adultery or some other sin. This is not a day of cheap grace. Judgment has already begun in the house of the Lord.

Many people are not living in the realm of the Holy Spirit. They are running around with familiar spirits and having visions that come from some place other than heaven. The Lord gave many of us a mandate to deal with these things in a very bold and plain way because we are not facing a generation that takes hints. They will not listen. Things must be said boldly by the Holy Spirit in a way to get their attention.

Living in the realm of the Holy Spirit — in the realm of miracles and power — is not like running in a hundred-yard dash with its quick sprint and emotional high. No, it is more like a marathon. The only way you are going to win this race is to decide to run no matter what comes and no matter what goes. It takes commitment to stay in there and keep putting one foot in front of the other.

It is time to get ready for the new move and time to get in it. If you want to be part of the revival, this book will help you get ready. It will help you press in to that place in God where the supernatural is natural.

Chapter 1

Heeding God's Voice

The calling voice of God comes to every generation, questioning and searching for the response that brings divine satisfaction.

In the Garden of Eden, His voice rang out, **Where art thou?** (Genesis 3:9).

In Abraham's day, God was calling for separation unto Him. (See Genesis 12:1.)

In Samuel's first years as a child ministering to the Lord before Eli, God was calling for holiness in the priests so His Spirit might be restored in the tabernacle. (See 1 Samuel 3.)

In Ezekiel's time, God was calling for an intercessor, one to stand in the gap between His mercy and judgment and to call for His grace. (See Ezekiel 22:30.)

In Nehemiah's generation, God's voice called for restoration, for the city of Jerusalem to be rebuilt, and for the nation of Judah to be restored as a people. (See Nehemiah 13:5.)

Today, God is calling us to holiness as He did in the days of Samuel. So many churches are standing far from the shore of Holy Spirit revival. They are fooled by material success into thinking they have achieved spiritual success. Where they once desired spiritual meat, now they eat from the minds of men — soul junk food. The hunger of God's people for spiritual food must be answered by today's leadership.

Yes, we preachers will be held accountable for such action. You may think I am being harsh or critical; however, I am not being judgmental. I am simply stating the facts and including myself in the warning.

Many spiritual leaders will stand before God on that great day of judgment and desire to have another opportunity to answer the Lord's call of bringing revival to the many soul-led and sin-bound churches of today just as Samuel brought Israel from spiritual decay to a tremendous revival.

God has never quit calling His people to live a life of purity and holiness, but today His voice is coming with strength, even as a roar. Let us humble ourselves before Him and help a needy generation. Let Jesus be seen instead of ourselves. God alone is the answer to any problem a believer has. We, in our own capability, cannot help anyone. Our job is to point them to Jesus by letting Jesus be first in our lives.

GOD IS CALLING THOSE WHO WILL HEAR AND OBEY

Today's situation is similar to the days of Samuel.

And the child Samuel ministered unto the Lord before Eli. And the word of the Lord was precious [valuable because it was scarce] in those days; there was no open vision.

And it came to pass at that time, when Eli was laid down in his place, and his eyes began to wax dim, that he could not see;

And ere the lamp of God went out in the temple of the Lord, where the ark of God was, and Samuel was laid down to sleep;

That the Lord called Samuel: and he answered, Here am I.

And he ran unto Eli, and said, Here am I; for thou calledst me. And he said, I called not; lie down again. And he went and lay down.

And the Lord called yet again, Samuel. And Samuel arose and went to Eli, and said, Here am I; for thou didst call me. And he answered, I called not, my son; lie down again.

Now Samuel did not yet know the Lord, neither was the word of the Lord yet revealed unto him.

And the Lord called Samuel again the third time. And he arose and went to Eli, and said, Here am I; for thou didst call me. And Eli perceived that the Lord had called the child.

1 Samuel 3:1-8 (author's insert)

Eli was supposed to be a great prophet. He was the high priest for all of Israel, the one who ministered to the Lord before the Ark of the Covenant. He was supposed to hear God and lead

His people in the ways God commanded. Yet Eli's home was a mess like many of today's prophets' homes are a mess.

The sons of Eli, who served as priests under his authority, were fornicating at the doors of the temple. They were stealing and doing all sorts of evil, and Eli did not have the backbone to compel them to change. He admonished them, but he did not speak with the authority of a father or a high priest. (See 1 Samuel 2:12-25.) If a man cannot rebuke his own sons, how is he going to confront God's people who are going the wrong way and bring the needed correction?

In the days of Samuel, there was no *open vision,* which meant there was no growth of God's revelation, or God's vision. Sadly, many of our churches today operate with no open vision. I am not saying miracles don't happen today, but if we really *heard* and *obeyed* the Holy Spirit, we would see a consistent flow of miracles.

Not many people know the voice of God because their "perceivers" are rusty, just like Eli's. They are trying to function in the realm of the spirit with their natural minds, and that will not work. They have a lot of "head knowledge" about the Bible, which does them little good, but their hearts are not full of the Word. The Word planted in the heart is what bears fruit, but we must rid our heads of pride and *religious* beliefs.

A POLISHED IMAGE

Once I was viewing a fine-tuned ministry of helps. I believed in this ministry and saw the great need for it, but the Spirit of the Lord spoke to me so strongly that it was like a roar. He said, "Excellence of ministry they have. Excellence of spirit they have not." Those words still echo in my heart. One of my board members put it so well when he said, "High gloss versus real substance."

Ministers have been so concerned about their image and the way they are perceived by the world that they spend more of their time developing outward aspects of their ministry than their relationships with the Lord. They are so busy keeping their ministry *highly glossed* that they lose their *real substance.* Will a marketable image without God's Word or God's anointing bring the harvest in for Jesus? Certainly not!

There are also those who are so concerned over spiritual excesses they cannot see where the real excesses are. They cannot see the forest for the trees. They are trying to keep God's people in low gear in order to monitor every little sign of supernatural manifestation, but where are the sermons that expose excesses of soulish activity in the Church? That should be their priority. It is better to have some spiritual "wildfire" than no fire at all! A minister who allows Jesus to flow through him will win his community to the Lord.

OPERATING ON GOD'S TERMS

John the Baptist went into all the country delivering God's perfect prophetic Word, regardless of who it hit and regardless of who received it and who did not. His only concern was the

Word. He did not allow people's feelings to weaken his message or adjust his position. He operated on God's terms, not man's.

The Lord convicted me one evening as I was preaching. There was a strong prophetic anointing, and the words coming out of my spirit were so exact that they were dividing soul from spirit. (See Hebrews 4:12.) I actually began to feel a wave of opposition coming toward me in the pulpit. I was shocked! To be honest, it scared me. I knew the people in the congregation so well that I could not believe the reaction I was getting. I began to translate God's words into my own choice of words to lessen the blow of opposition I felt. I changed His words to those I thought were less offensive, but my words did not carry the same weight as those the Lord used. John the Baptist spoke the Lord's words exactly. His message angered the leaders of his day and so will ours.

That evening, the Holy Spirit quickly rebuked me. He said, "Who are you to change My words and make them attractive to the soul? My words bring separation and clarity to the hungry and conviction to others. Don't be afraid of that which you feel. Speak as you are spoken to."

John the Baptist said, **He [Jesus] must increase, but I must decrease** (John 3:30).

Are we willing to say that and mean it? Are we willing to allow the Holy Spirit to move freely in our lives to accomplish the work He has planned for us? If so, we must decrease in our own selfish wants and desires and only want that which the Lord wants. It's not always easy because it involves a dying to our flesh. But it is always worth it!

THE MESSAGE TO LAODICEA

The message to the church at Laodicea could very well have been written to many churches today.

Behold, I stand at the door, and knock: if any man hear my voice, and open the door, I will come in to him, and will sup with him, and he with me.

Revelation 3:20

Is Jesus standing at the door of your life and ministry trying to get in? Is Jesus allowed to move as He wills in your church? There are so many churches today whose personalities are based on their pastor's personality. Many ministers are diverting the attention of the sheep from the Chief Shepherd to themselves, and many have a great following.

Yes, there is always personality involved because God works in cooperation with His children. But He wants them to be so conformed to the image of His dear Son that their character is like that of Jesus.

And be not conformed to this world: but be ye transformed by the renewing of your mind, that ye may prove what is that good, and acceptable, and perfect, will of God.

Romans 12:2

On the other hand, many great leaders warn people not to follow them but to look to Jesus, yet some of the sheep insist on keeping their eyes on the pastor or minister. That is idolatry, and it is one of man's greatest temptations. Idolatry is putting anything between you and Jesus. It might be money, possessions, your spouse or children, or spiritual leaders, and if your focus and greatest love are on them instead of the Lord, you are verging on idolatry.

John the Baptist had a strong personality to the point that the Bible even records the kind of clothes he wore. However, what stirred the country was not his taste in clothes or his personality, but his message. He subordinated his personality so the Word of the Lord could be heard and seen.

John the Baptist began decreasing after Jesus' ministry began in order for Jesus to increase. He did the best he could to get out of the limelight. Let us take an example from him. Do not build an empire where Jesus is not number one. Build your ministry on Jesus and not on yourself. We don't need Hollywood-style preachers. We can't afford for our primary concern to be the offerings rather than the messages. We don't have time to build ministries on something other than Jesus. Let us commit to working for God on His terms.

THE ABILITY TO HEAR GOD

Notice who God spoke to when He decided it was time to do something about Eli and his wicked sons — a little boy whose mother cried out one day and said, "God, I need a son. If You will give me a son, I will give him back to You to serve You all the days of his life." (See 1 Samuel 1:11.)

God answered her prayer, and when Samuel was weaned his mother brought him to Eli to serve the Lord as she had promised. (See 1 Samuel 1:24-28.) Samuel grew in the grace of the Lord and found joy in serving the old prophet. He was a simple little boy who loved God.

When the calling voice of God came to Samuel, he did not recognize it because the voice of the Lord was not heard around the tabernacle anymore. This was something new to him. When he heard his name called, it was usually Eli telling him to do something. So three times when he heard, "Samuel, Samuel," he went running to Eli, who finally realized the Lord must be speaking.

Therefore Eli said unto Samuel, Go, lie down: and it shall be, if he call thee, that thou shalt say, Speak, Lord; for thy servant heareth. So Samuel went and lay down in his place.

And the Lord came, and stood, and called as at other times, Samuel, Samuel. Then Samuel answered, Speak; for they servant heareth.

And the Lord said to Samuel, Behold, I will do a thing in Israel, at which both the ears of every one that heareth it shall tingle.

In that day I will perform against Eli all things which I have spoken concerning his house: when I begin, I will also make an end.

For I have told him that I will judge his house for ever for the iniquity which he knoweth; because his sons made themselves vile, and he restrained them not.

And therefore I have sworn unto the house of Eli, that the iniquity of Eli's house shall not be purged with sacrifice nor offering for ever.

And Samuel lay until the morning, and opened the doors of the house of the Lord. And Samuel feared to show Eli the vision.

Then Eli called Samuel, and said, Samuel, my son. And he answered, Here am I.

And he said, What is the thing that the Lord hath said unto thee? I pray thee hide it not from me: God do so to thee, and more also, if thou hide any thing from me of all the things that he said unto thee.

And Samuel told him every whit, and hid nothing from him. And he said, It is the Lord: let him do what seemeth him good.

1 Samuel 3:9-18

Samuel was nervous about telling Eli what the Lord had said, but he was obedient and repeated the message exactly. He did not try to paraphrase it or soften it — he gave it straight. Eli confirmed that the Lord indeed had spoken.

And Samuel grew, and the Lord was with him, and did let none of his words fall to the ground.

> And all Israel from Dan even to Beersheba knew that
> Samuel was established to be a prophet of the Lord.
>
> 1 Samuel 3:19-20

Samuel was confirmed as a prophet of the Lord while he was still young. God is not waiting for you to get an education or have a big bank account. He is not waiting for you to get to a certain age or a certain place. God is not looking for mental agreement alone, but for a heart that says, "Speak and I will listen. I will obey You. I am Your servant."

WHO WILL ANSWER THE CALL?

The voice of God is saying, "I need someone who will stand up against the flow of this world — against the pride, lethargy, and fakery in the Church, and say, 'No!' I am looking for those who will show forth the glory of the Lord in the earth today."

God is calling those who will do what He says when He says and not ask why. He needs generals in His army. He needs sergeants to train the rank and file. He needs captains who will stand up against the stubbornness of some church leaders and against the laziness in some pews. He is looking for those who will confront the sons of Eli and say, "This is the way the Lord says we shall go, and if you don't go this way, then what comes to you is your own fault."

> So then they that are in the flesh cannot please God.
>
> Romans 8:8

235

This journey cannot be made with your flesh untouched. Flesh must be under divine control from your spirit man. The Church must come back into the realm of the Spirit and the realm of real faith. God does not need any more hype. He does not need any more soulish ministry masquerading as something spiritual. The things of the flesh must be cut off and exposed, allowing the truth to come forth.

God is giving a fresh anointing to those who will receive it. His voice is going through every home and every church in the world. His voice is going to every ear in the world — saint or sinner — and is being heard by young and old, whether it is recognized or not.

God's voice is not asking what you know but, "Are you willing? Will you yield your life to Me? Will you give up the things of this world — the weights and the anchors of this world that hold you down — and come away with Me? Come into the spirit realm that I have made for you. I will carry you and show you the glory I have waiting for you."

I believe this revival of God has come as close as it is going to come. We must now reach up and turn loose of all the weights and anchors. We must begin to journey. We must travel without looking back and without saying, "Lord, my friends aren't coming. My relatives aren't coming."

We cannot look at all of these people. We must look unto the Author and Finisher of our faith and journey closer to Him.

Remain in the truth you have learned, but never stay behind. Many men and women are missing their visitations from heaven because they are not following the voice of the Lord, but rather some man or some doctrine that will not endure the fire of God.

One evening the Lord spoke this prophecy:

The ability of God shall rise up out of you, and you shall hear with your own ears the voice of the Lord coming out, and you will learn as you speak. You will learn as I begin to flow out of you because that is one of the greatest schools I have implemented in the Church — the school of My Spirit. Men may say and men may do, but my Spirit knows it all.

So this day, lean not on your own understanding and lean not to the right or to the left, nor to the front or the back, but look up and go that way. For the calling voice of God is coming and has come unto you, and you must learn that when you answer that call and when you begin to journey on this road to a higher place and higher realm, all hell will try to stop you. But understand this: The gates of hell shall not prevail against the kingdom of God that is within you!

Remember, there are no excuses in God's court. You cannot say you are too young or too old, you do not know enough, or you do not have enough time. Open your heart and allow God to put within you the ability and the grace to be established in the earth. He will give you the ability and the strength to do what He has called you to do.

The world may stand back and say, "Who are you, and where did you come from?"

And you will be able to reply, "I am a man (or woman) of God, and I am equipped with the ability of God, not of men."

He who began a good work in you will perfect it until the day of Christ Jesus.

Philippians 1:6 NASB

CHAPTER 2

ARE YOU READY TO SUBDUE KINGDOMS?

> And what more shall I say? For time will fail me if I tell of Gideon, Barak, Samson, Jephthah, of David and Samuel and the prophets,
>
> Who by faith conquered kingdoms, performed acts of righteousness, obtained promises, shut the mouth of lions,
>
> Quenched the power of fire, escaped the edge of the sword, from weakness were made strong, became mighty in war, put foreign armies to flight.
>
> **Hebrews 11:32-34** NASB

God gave us faith so we could conquer or subdue kingdoms and bring forth righteousness. We are supposed to overcome kingdoms and bring them into submission to the hand or will of God. (See Matthew 6:10.)

When I got back from my trip to Africa in 1984, the Lord kept bringing the phrase **who through faith subdued kingdoms** (Hebrews 11:33) to me. I have studied Church history for many years and read about preachers who could take their communities or cities for the Lord. Some could take several cities in one move, while others could take a whole nation. The Bible records a number of people who were subduers of nations.

Not long ago, I returned from a preaching tour in Europe. It is no longer a place where darkness rules. The light has begun to shine. What God is doing in Europe and other nations is wonderful, and what He is doing in our country is wonderful. The United States will not go under if we humble ourselves before Him in prayer and answer the calling voice of God in our generation.

God did not call us to hide in a corner. He called us to be bold and out in the open. We're to make people nervous in a positive way as John the Baptist did and say what the Holy Spirit says. He did not call us to try to keep from offending anyone. When we got saved, we enlisted in an army — God's army. If you belong to the body of Christ, you are in some degree of spiritual warfare. God did not call us to *tolerate* the devil and his works. He called us to *destroy* the works of the devil.

> **And the angel of the Lord appeared unto him [Gideon], and said unto him, The Lord is with thee, thou mighty man of valour.**
>
> **Judges 6:12 (author's insert)**

Gideon is a good example. Like most of us, he did not believe he was a "mighty man of valor." At the time the angel appeared, he was hiding some of his produce from the Midianites because they had overrun the land. Gideon wanted to know why the enemies of Israel had run over them if the Lord truly was with them.

That is what many of us are saying. "If God truly is with us, why are all these things happening?" The answer is the same today as it was then. These things happen because the enemy — the Midianites in Gideon's day and the devil in ours — has not been pushed out of our territory. We can't rule our territory when our enemy is occupying the land.

Revival is a divine attack on Satan's rule in society. We are called to invade every aspect of satanic influence. God never called His Church to go out and take people out of the world, put them in a quiet little corner, and tell them, "Now stay there until Jesus comes."

Jesus never meant for us to look at the rapture of the Church as an escape route. When He returns, we are to be found working and *occupying*. He did not call us to hide and be silent. When He returns, we ought to be busy obeying His directions, which may be building new churches, putting new ministries on television and radio, writing new books, or moving out in new evangelistic campaigns around the world. Our efforts to advance the kingdom of God do not end until He says they do.

THE LORD IS A FIGHTER

The Lord is a warrior and a fighter. We desperately need a revelation of that part of His character. For so long, Jesus was presented as a wimpy, meek-and-mild man, when He really was the opposite. He had to be bold and assertive to walk through the religious society and the civil structure of His day. But He was concerned with speaking only what His Father said. He was not concerned with the reactions of men.

And where be all his miracles which our fathers told us of, saying, Did not the Lord bring us up from Egypt? but now the Lord hath forsaken us, and delivered us into the hands of the Midianites.

Judges 6:13

Many Christians are looking at their towns and cities and saying, "When is God going to move? Where are all of the miracles our fathers told us of in generations past?"

God is waiting for Gideons. When He finds someone who will be a Gideon, He will move. The Lord looked at Gideon and said, "Go." He did not tell Gideon to sit down and talk about it or to wait for a better time. He said, "Gideon, you go and save Israel from the hand of the Midianites."

Gideon had a lot of excuses, just as we have — his family was poor and among his family he was "the least." He was afraid. But God did not accept his excuses. He did not feel sorry for Gideon and find someone else.

And the Lord said unto him, Surely I will be with thee, and thou shalt smite the Midianites as one man.

Judges 6:16

You can be a one-man army. That is what the great spiritual leaders of the past were. When Billy Sunday came to town, the saloons went out of business. We must put aside our accom-modation-of-the-world thinking.

Love has two sides — unconditional acceptance and divine confrontation. Unconditional permissiveness is not love. "Sloppy agape" is not love. "Cheap grace" is not love. When Jesus cleansed the temple, He did not walk in there to gently and politely ask the moneychangers to leave. No, He strode in there with a whip in His hand and truth on His lips. He loudly spoke out the will of the Father. (See Mark 11:15-17.) If that happened in our day, a lot of church people would say Jesus was arrogant, rude, and not walking in love!

God is bringing a more balanced understanding of the love walk. Many who were influenced by the rebellious atmosphere of the sixties have mistaken love for license. Love is not the freedom to do whatever we want, whatever our flesh wants. Love is doing what is right in God's sight because God is love.

CONFRONTING EVIL

Jesus went about doing good — healing the sick, delivering the oppressed, and teaching the poor. He did not teach them how to "cope with life." He taught them how to confront evil, not compro-mise with it. Too many preachers today say, "Let's walk in love," and ignore the other side of love, which is divine confrontation.

The Lord gave me a vision once of many crippled and other-wise handicapped people. I was excited, thinking that a great miracle ministry had come to me. Then the Lord said, "That's not what I am showing you. These are spiritual handicaps and spiritual conditions. These things come because My people do not know how to fight. Go to the churches where I open doors, and do not be just a teacher. Be a commander and a trainer! Show them how to fight the devil and enjoy it. My Church is in warfare. You are not there to live casually. You are in a deep battle for eternal purposes."

The warfare, the spiritual conflicts God has for us to be involved in, cannot be done in a corner. (See Acts 26:26.) Paul was a militant man, and we must be militant in our day. Warfare and revival — the divine attack on society — in any day is not done in a corner. God said it is done out in the open for all to hear and receive.

We must move from fighting the devil defensively to fighting him offensively. Our goal can no longer be simply to survive. It is time to take back our territory and attack the gates of hell. When I go into a city or a nation, I look out the airplane window on the way down and begin to pray for the people there, binding the principalities that rule over the people and over their nation.

You have to live that way in God's army. You have to know that every place the sole of your foot touches is yours and God's. Isaiah 11:9 says, **The earth shall be full of the knowledge of the Lord.** That knowledge is not going to come trickling down, but it will be as the waters that cover the sea, and we are going to be the carriers of it. We are called to stir up the world and to turn it upside down. (See Acts 17:6.) We're not to breeze through the world simply being pleasant, nice Christians.

Many more Christians would be willing to go into the mission field if that mission field were Hawaii, but God does not always call you to a place you like! Sometimes that is to keep you from getting caught up in the leisure activities of that place. If you are not caught up in the scenery, you will be quicker to do the bidding of the Lord.

He sent me to the north, and I am a southerner. Weather in the north is not exciting to me. It snows too much and gets too cold! But the Lord said, "I want you to fight the principalities of the north," and I said, "but what about the principalities of the south — like Florida?"

The principalities of my hometown, Tulsa, Oklahoma, are not as strong as other places. They have been beaten up really well and do not move as they used to move. The demonic power is not as strong there as it is in other places. However, wherever we are, our fight is against principalities and demonic forces, not against other men.

> **For we wrestle not against flesh and blood, but against principalities, against powers, against the rulers of the darkness of this world, against spiritual wickedness in high places.**
>
> **Ephesians 6:12**

The warrior attitude is this: *Never give up.* When Elisha asked God to open the eyes of his servant to see that there was more help on their side than on the enemy's, the servant saw a ring of warring angels. They had swords in their hands, not harps. (See 2 Kings 6:16-17.) Today is no different. In fact, we have it better. Not only do we have warring angels on our side, we also have the authority and the ability to go forth in the power of the Holy Spirit.

IT IS TIME TO SUBDUE NATIONS

Some time ago, God began to speak to me that this is the season for men and women to subdue nations, bring righteousness, and obtain His promises. Too many of us look at a city and see its might, but this is not the day to be satisfied with cities. It is time that we begin to look at countries. It is time to look at the impossibilities and grin because we know we are going to win!

Of course there is a fight. We need to be forceful to subdue kingdoms. Matthew 11:12 says, **The kingdom of heaven suffereth violence, and the violent take it by force.** The *New International Version* translates it as **the kingdom of heaven has been forcefully advancing, and forceful men lay hold of it.** Another, Moffatt, translates it as **they are pressing into the Realm of heaven — these eager souls are storming it!**

THE FIRST KEY IS OBEDIENCE

The first key to subduing kingdoms is *obedience*. We must learn to obey the voice of God. One reason so many believers have never been able to succeed is because they have not learned to be obedient to God.

When I was eleven years old, God called me to preach. He said, "Will you preach for Me today?"

I said, "God, I haven't even finished high school yet."

He said, "If you will follow Me and start preaching, I will give you an education that you wouldn't receive anywhere else."

I said, "God, I'll go. I'll do it. I don't care what You want me to do, where You want me to go, or what You want me to say when I get there — I'll do it."

In 1983, God said, "I want you to go to Moscow this year."

I said, "I want to go to some other nation in Europe, God."

"I don't want you to go to some other nation in Europe. You have to go to Moscow."

"What in the world for?"

He told me to be quiet and go.

"If you want me to go," I said, "You just cause it." He did. He sent the money and had two ministers invite me to go with them. I did not want to go to Russia, but I chose to obey God. When I told the Lord I would go, it became a desire within me. The thought of going to Moscow was exciting and fun, and I was able to go with the joy of the Lord.

We flew to Helsinki, Finland, where we met with people who were arranging our contacts inside Russia. That evening, we flew into Moscow. When we crossed the border between

Finland and Russia, we did not need an announcement from the pilot. We knew it because we could feel the oppression of the demonic spirits there.

If you are going to subdue a nation, you have to go behind enemy lines and attack from that side. You have to be cunning and wise in the spirit because there is a battle raging out there. Do not even try it if you are not sure you are hearing the voice of the Lord, or if you are not willing to be completely obedient.

God spoke to us during dinner and said, "This night you go to Red Square and prophesy to the walls."

I thought, "Lord, You know that is not supposed to be done — especially by American tourists."

He said, "You go and I will tell you what to do."

When we got to our hotel, our bodies were suffering from jet lag and screaming for bed, but our spirits kept saying, "Go, go, go!" We yielded to the Spirit, and God said, "Get on the subway."

None of us could read a bit of Russian, and there were not too many people on the streets at night who could speak English, but our group obediently took the subway to Red Square. There the Spirit of God began to speak to us to prophesy to the walls.

The Lord said, "You walk that square seven times. Seven times you walk, and you prophesy. You prophesy to the red star. You prophesy and send My angels into the place where the president works."

We went to an underground church and talked with a man involved in the underground press in one region of Russia. Over lunch at his home, he shared what was happening among God's people behind the Iron Curtain. After that trip I said that Russia would see a great revival, and we are now seeing it come to pass. The Iron Curtain has been torn down, the country is more open to the Gospel, and large numbers of people are coming to the Lord. Hallelujah!

THE SECOND KEY IS THE POWER OF PRAYER

The effectual fervent prayer of a righteous man availeth much.

James 5:16

The second key to subduing nations is *learning the power of prayer.* When you get down on your knees and open yourself in prayer for God to move through you, you must be totally yielded to have perfect success. A religious routine will get you nowhere. The demons will say, "Ha, ha, ha. We're not budging — you are." So you must learn how to pray without quitting. Nice little prayers will not move you into the realm where devils quake and mountains move. They will not get you to that place where signs and wonders flow. You must hook up to the vast power of God and persevere until the victory is won.

The devil declares war on you when you start praying. He assigns special warriors to come against you. He does things to try to stop you from praying. If he can keep believers from praying, he has the world under his control.

The name of Jesus is powerful, but you must enforce it. You have to hit the devils with it. You have to fight them with His most excellent name. If you take the attitude of, *I'm going to win or die fighting,* the devils will be afraid of you and flee when you come on the scene.

God gave me a clear picture of the kinds of battles that are taking place for whole nations when I flew into Zimbabwe some time ago. God said, "Come up hither, and let Me take you to a battle." He pulled me up into the spirit realm and took me to a place where I could see the fighting without being involved in the battle.

He said, "I want you to view it before we go into it. This is the battle for the nation of Zimbabwe."

I had seen battles for individuals, for families, for financial situations, and for ministries, but this was the first time I had ever seen a real battle where angels and devils were fighting directly. I saw huge, powerful creatures out there going around and around with huge, powerful angels — fighting, wrestling, and warring on the battlefield.

We have to bring down the demonic princes over cities and nations. We have to hit the devil when he tries to walk up to us. Do not wait for him to hit you first. Sock it to him! Be determined to do something for God. Be determined to win!

I do not understand believers who just pray a little bit, read a little bit, go to church a little bit, socialize a little bit, hit a little bit, and forgive a little bit. They are of little use to the kingdom of God. They have not tapped in to the awesome power of Almighty God. They do not look at things with spiritual eyes; then they wonder why they never experience God and why they cannot hear the voice of the Lord. We must learn to move in the realm of the spirit.

OBEDIENCE BRINGS VICTORY AND BLESSINGS

When God called me, I committed to be obedient and to pray. The Lord tested my obedience in many little things before He brought me to the bigger things, and I spent hour upon hour in prayer that changed me and changed things in the spirit realm.

The trip to Russia was one of the big tests of obedience, but an even bigger test was when God told me to go to Africa. For some time before God first began to speak to me about going to Zimbabwe, the word *Zimbabwe* would come out when I was praying in tongues. I just thought it was another word in my prayer language and did not pay attention to it, until someone who had been praying with me said, "Did you know that Zimbabwe is a nation?"

I said, "No, where is it?"

"I don't know. I just know it is a nation."

I bought a world map and pinned it on the wall to look for Zimbabwe. When I got to the continent of Africa, the nation of

Zimbabwe enlarged itself about twenty times, and the only thing I could see was the nation of Zimbabwe.

God said, "Roberts, you are going to have to go to Zimbabwe the year you graduate from high school."

"God, I don't want to go to Zimbabwe," I said. "I want to go to Europe or some place civilized. You sent me to Moscow. It was nice, but it wasn't great."

He said, "You are going to go."

"You'll have to make it happen, or I won't go," I said. I did not give it much thought until God brought a man up to me at a convention in St. Louis.

"God spoke to me to invite you to come to my country this year," he said.

I said, "Well, all right, I will go."

After I agreed and accepted the desire for the African trip, God began to show me what to do. "You go to Rome, and you go to the Vatican," He said. "I want you to stay there a few hours."

I thought, *God, how are You going to arrange that with a flight schedule?*

"Just tell them that you want to go to Uganda as well."

"Why in the world do You want me to go to Uganda as well?"

Again, He told me to be quiet and go.

I called a travel agent and told him what I needed. He checked his computer and said it worked out perfectly. He booked our team on a flight to Rome with a thirteen-hour layover before flying to Uganda for six days, then on to Zimbabwe.

A few days after graduation, we took off for Rome. I went to the Vatican and walked and prophesied. I went inside and walked and prophesied until my spirit said, "You've done enough. Now go to the airport."

Then we went to Uganda.

God said, "I'll take you from the bottom of the nation to the top of the nation."

One of our team members, Akkiki Muyu, grew up in Uganda but had attended Oral Roberts University. She introduced us to a Full Gospel banker she knew. We were having a nice visit when the banker leaned back in his big chair and said, "I believe you need to see the president."

"I think I do too," I said, thinking he was joking.

"Do you want me to call him?"

"Sure."

He picked up the phone and called the president. "We have some American missionaries here who have been praying for you. You need to see them," he said.

We went to President Obote's office. I was a little nervous because I had never met the president of a nation before. I was praying, "God, You're going to have to help me. What am I going to say to him?"

The Lord said, "Remember when I called you to preach? I told you to open up your mouth and I would fill it. You do the same here. This is no different."

After President Obote and I exchanged greetings and were seated, the Spirit of prophecy fell on me. I have learned that when God starts moving, no matter who you are with, you had better go with Him. If you do not, you may find yourself in a predicament. No matter how strange it may look, go with God and everything will work out. So I began to let the words bubble up out of me.

"If you'll run your nation the right way, righteously before God, the nation will prosper and grow. If you do not run the nation righteously, judgment will come. Great disaster will be upon your land. God has sent me from America to pray for you, and to ask God to send His angels to be beside you to help you."

TIME IS SHORT

It is time to expand our vision and subdue nations. In fact, it is past time. Cities and regions are not enough. However, in order for us to move into that realm of the spirit, we must learn to obey, we must learn to pray, we must learn to yield ourselves to God, and we must learn to give up the things of the world. If God calls you to do something, forget everything else and give all your strength and might to that one thing.

The day is coming, and it is not far off, when there will be nations subdued by people of God — nations that have wrought righteousness and obtained the promises of God. There will be nations where devils have been driven out, and the ones who refused to go are bound so tightly no one will notice them. There will be nations where you will be able to feel the mighty rushing wind of the Spirit as soon as you step across the border.

Great things will happen in our day if the people of God will go out and subdue the nations through faith in God and by His supernatural power. God wants to use us in that way. Are you willing? Are you ready to stand back and watch the power of God be manifested throughout this earth?

Chapter 3

The Anointing
Is for Action

And it shall come to pass in that day, that his burden shall be taken away from off thy shoulder, and his yoke from off thy neck, and the yoke shall be destroyed because of the anointing.

Isaiah 10:27

The anointing breaks the yoke of bondage. The yoke of poverty is destroyed by the anointing. The yoke of sickness is destroyed by the anointing. Whatever the devil tries to put on us or send against us is destroyed by the anointing of God.

The anointing is not something spooky, and it is not solely for full-time ministers. The anointing is for the entire body of Christ. We need to put aside all the weird ideas we may have and learn to walk in His anointing every day — applying it in the practical operation of our everyday lives.

> And let the peace of God rule in your hearts, to the which also ye are called in one body; and be ye thankful.
>
> Colossians 3:15

There is no Hollywood in heaven, and there are no superstars in heaven. We are all called to be a particular part of the body of Christ and to flow together as one, but we cannot do it without the anointing of God. Unfortunately, the anointing and the understanding of the anointing are sadly lacking in many churches today.

What is the anointing? The anointing is the divine power God grants to a believer through the Holy Spirit to minister to the world and to the body of Christ.

> Now there are diversities of gifts, but the same Spirit.
>
> And there are differences of administrations, but the same Lord.
>
> And there are diversities of operations, but it is the same God which worketh all in all.
>
> But the manifestation of the Spirit is given to every man to profit withal.
>
> 1 Corinthians 12:4-7

Jesus is our example of ministering under the anointing. You may say, "That was easy — Jesus was the Son of God." That is true, but Jesus did not minister on the earth as the Son of God; He ministered as a man anointed by the Holy Spirit — the same thing He has called us to do.

How God anointed Jesus of Nazareth with the Holy Ghost and with power: who went about doing good, and healing all that were oppressed of the devil; for God was with him.

Acts 10:38

Jesus laid aside everything connected with being the Son of God and operated as a mere man whose power and authority came through the Holy Spirit. There would be no need for Him to be anointed if He were ministering as the Son of God.

Have this attitude in yourselves which was also in Christ Jesus,

Who, although He existed in the form of God, did not regard equality with God a thing to be grasped,

But emptied Himself, taking the form of a bond-servant, and being made in the likeness of men.

And being found in appearance as a man, He humbled Himself by becoming obedient to the point of death, even death on a cross.

Philippians 2:5-8 NASB

JESUS WAS ANOINTED FOR ACTION

The Bible records the beginning of Jesus' earthly ministry in chapters 3 and 4 of Luke. Jesus went to John the Baptist to be baptized, and as Jesus prayed, heaven was opened and the Holy Ghost descended in a bodily shape like a dove upon Him. (See Luke 3:21-22.) The Holy Spirit then led Jesus into the wilderness for a forty-day fast, during which time He was tempted by the devil. Using the Word of God as His only weapon, Jesus resisted all that the enemy sent against Him to try to stop His ministry. Instead, scripture tells us:

> Jesus returned in the power of the Spirit....
>
> And he came to Nazareth, where he had been brought up: and, as his custom was, he went into the synagogue on the sabbath day, and stood up for to read.
>
> And there was delivered unto him the book of the prophet Esaias [Isaiah]. And when he had opened the book, he found the place where it was written,
>
> The Spirit of the Lord is upon me, because he hath anointed me to preach the gospel to the poor; he hath sent me to heal the brokenhearted, to preach deliverance to the captives, and recovering of sight to the blind, to set at liberty them that are bruised,
>
> To preach the acceptable year of the Lord.
>
> Luke 4:14,16-19

Jesus was anointed to:

- preach the Gospel to the poor.
- heal the brokenhearted.
- preach deliverance to the captives.
- preach recovering of sight to the blind.
- set at liberty them that are bruised.
- preach the acceptable year of the Lord.

Notice that each item begins with a verb — an *action* word. Jesus was anointed for action. He was a man of bold action. Jesus was not anointed to take a defensive posture. Each of the actions listed was a bold thrust against the enemy. Each was an offensive move to drive the enemy out of the lives of God's people.

The Gospel to the poor is that they do not have to be poor anymore! There is an anointing that will break the yoke of poverty over them. This anointing works anywhere in the world. The Gospel is not just for North America. It is the Gospel of the kingdom of God. When the poor are taught to give unto the Lord, God will bless them, and the spirits of poverty and lack will be driven out of their lives as well as out of entire regions.

Healing the brokenhearted does not mean joining them in a pity party. Healing comes when things are boldly dealt with, even if it hurts. If an arm or a leg needs stitches, it will hurt in the beginning but be a blessing in the long run. Jesus was compassionate — but bold — in dealing with the source of the problem. He cast out spirits of self-pity, grief, and sorrow.

What is *preaching deliverance to the captives?* The Lord showed me a vision once of people in a cage, and they all had weird smiles. The Lord said, "Go up there and look at them. This is what many of My churches are like."

I went and saw there were also people walking by outside the cage. I looked more closely and realized that the people in the cage thought they were free and thought the people outside were in captivity! They were deceived into thinking that captivity was freedom!

Preaching deliverance to captives is boldly speaking the truth in love and breaking the bondage of deception. That takes the strength and anointing of the Holy Spirit. The Church needs this kind of preaching because so many believers are held captive by sickness, the flesh, soulish theology, the past, and bitterness. Many are deceived and ignorant of the enemy's devices. The anointing of God blasts through those deceptions and brings the liberty of truth into a person's life.

And ye shall know the truth, and the truth shall make you free.

John 8:32

To preach recovery of sight to the blind includes both natural and spiritual blindness. Jesus opened blind *physical* eyes and blind *spiritual* eyes. Your physical eyes are valuable, but the eyes of the spirit are more important. In this day of great spiritual activity, if you have no discernment and cannot operate in the realm of the spirit, you will be bound. Christians need to see things as God sees them. When our spiritual eyes are open and focused on the Lord, He will show us what we are to do and where we are to go, both individually and corporately.

To set at liberty them that are bruised requires tremendous strength and anointing. The Greek word translated for bruised does not mean a little black-and-blue mark you might get from bumping into something. It is the word *thrauo*, which means "crushed, shattered to minute pieces." (See James Strong's *The*

Exhaustive Concordance of the Bible (Nashville: Abingdon, 1890), "Greek Dictionary of the New Testament," #2352.) People crushed by the enemy need help from anointed ministers of God to receive healing and deliverance. The anointing will help put their lives back together according to the Word and teach them to stand against the devil.

Preaching the acceptable year of the Lord is preaching the timings and seasons of God. We need to be aware of what God is doing in the earth and flow with Him as He directs. Right now, I believe the season is changing. We are seeing God work in a different way from what we have become accustomed to. We have been in a teaching season, but I believe we are moving into a preaching season. The teacher lays out points — one, two, three — but the preacher comes in with boldness and goes *kaboom!* The preacher must know how to flow in the anointing, or he is a big loud "boom" that means nothing. I believe preaching will be a part of God's weaponry against the devil in these last days.

THE POWER TO DO GOOD

As Jesus ministered in the earth under the anointing of the Holy Spirit, He took bold action against the works of the enemy. He ministered in the power and authority of the Holy Spirit. (See Acts 10:38.)

Everywhere Jesus went, the anointing and power went with Him to heal, to deliver, to set free, and to destroy the works of the devil. This was Jesus' purpose on this earth. (See 1 John 3:8.)

He was ministering under the anointing when He blessed the children and when He drove the moneychangers out of the temple. He was anointed when He fed the five thousand and when He cast out demons. He went about doing good for people and blasting the devil.

The anointing was for Jesus' ministry, but it was not for His day-to-day living. He walked by faith in the everyday affairs of life. He did not try to live in the anointing.

> **And when he had sent the multitudes away, he went up into a mountain apart to pray: and when the evening was come, he was there alone.**
>
> **Matthew 14:23**

Jesus regularly separated Himself from others to pray and fellowship with the Father. That is when He got His "marching orders." There was no independent action in Jesus' life. His personal life was based on prayer and absolute obedience and submission to the Father. He prayed to the Father in faith, heard what the Father said, then went out and did what the Father said to do — all under the anointing of the Holy Spirit. Jesus said:

> **For I have not spoken of myself; but the Father which sent me, he gave me a commandment, what I should say, and what I should speak.**
>
> **And I know that his commandment is life everlasting: whatsoever I speak therefore, even as the Father said unto me, so I speak.**
>
> **John 12:49-50**

We can see from the life of Jesus that the anointing is for ministry to people. Also, the anointing is a mighty weapon against the enemy — a forward thrust to destroy the works of the devil, not just a defensive weapon to ward off attack. The anointing sets people free and defeats the enemy. The anointing breaks the yoke of bondage. It is the power to change things.

The anointing is for service and not for show. Jesus did not use the anointing to become a superstar. He ministered to the needs of the people. He did not use the anointing for personal gain or His own private affairs. It was for the public and before the public.

The anointing was not the dominant factor in Jesus' life. The dominant factor was His relationship with the Father. The anointing is important, but it is not the most important thing in life — our relationship with God is.

The anointing is for everyone in the body of Christ. Ecclesiastes 9:8 says, **Let thy head lack no ointment,** or anointing. We need the anointing to do the will of God because we cannot do it out of the flesh. We cannot meet the needs of other people in our own strength and ability. It must be by the anointing of the Holy Spirit.

> **Not by might, nor by power, but by my spirit, saith the Lord of hosts.**
>
> Zechariah 4:6

LUCIFER – THE ANOINTED CHERUB

There was a day when the devil was good. He was in heaven and mightily anointed by God, but he made a wrong choice.

Thou hast been in Eden the garden of God; every precious stone was thy covering, the sardius, topaz, and the diamond, the beryl, the onyx, and the jasper, the sapphire, the emerald, and the carbuncle, and gold: the workmanship of thy tabrets and of thy pipes was prepared in thee in the day that thou wast created.

Thou are the anointed cherub that covereth; and I have set thee so: thou wast upon the holy mountain of God; thou hast walked up and down in the midst of the stones of fire.

Thou wast perfect in thy ways from the day that thou wast created, till iniquity was found in thee.

By the multitude of thy merchandise they have filled the midst of thee with violence, and thou hast sinned: therefore I will cast thee as profane out of the mountain of God: and I will destroy thee, O covering cherub, from the midst of the stones of fire.

Thine heart was lifted up because of thy beauty, thou hast corrupted thy wisdom by reason of thy brightness: I will cast thee to the ground, I will lay thee before kings, that they may behold thee.

Thou hast defiled thy sanctuaries by the multitude of thine iniquities; by the iniquity of thy traffick; therefore will I bring forth a fire from the midst of thee, it shall devour thee, and I will bring thee to ashes upon the earth in the sight of all them that behold thee.

Ezekiel 28:13-18

Lucifer was the anointed cherub that covered. God created him perfect and set him upon His holy mountain. He had great wisdom and sat right next to God. His beauty was beyond description, with every precious stone as his covering. His beauty was not just for the eyes but also for the ears because he was in charge of the music of heaven. The musical instruments — tabrets and pipes — were within him.

COVETING THE GLORY

Lucifer had it made. He was under the anointing. He still understands the anointing and knows what kind of power the anointing brings. He hates anyone who has the anointing because he lost it. His heart was lifted up in pride because of his beauty and his position. *Pride covets the glory that belongs only to God.* God will not share His glory with anyone. The pride in Lucifer opened the door to self-will and rebellion.

How art thou fallen from heaven, O Lucifer, son of the morning! how art thou cut down to the ground, which didst weaken the nations!

For thou hast said in thine heart, I will ascend into heaven, I will exalt my throne above the stars of God: I will sit also upon the mount of the congregation, in the sides of the north:

I will ascend above the heights of the clouds; I will be like the most High.

Yet thou shalt be brought down to hell, to the sides of the pit.

> They that see thee shall narrowly look upon thee,
> and consider thee, saying, Is this the man that made the
> earth to tremble, that did shake kingdoms;
>
> That made the world as a wilderness, and destroyed
> the cities thereof; that opened not the house of his
> prisoners?
>
> Isaiah 14:12-17

Notice all the "I wills" in those verses. Pride swelled in Lucifer's heart. He wanted the glory, so he decided to exalt himself and be like God. That decision was one of self-will. He put himself and what he wanted above God's will and entered into rebellion and treason. He came against the authority of God. When you touch authority, you touch God Himself because He is authority. Of course, God could not allow Lucifer to do what he planned, so there was war in heaven.

> And there was war in heaven: Michael and his angels
> fought against the dragon; and the dragon fought and
> his angels,
>
> And prevailed not; neither was their place found any
> more in heaven.
>
> And the great dragon was cast out, that old serpent,
> called the Devil, and Satan, which deceiveth the whole
> world: he was cast out into the earth, and his angels
> were cast out with him.
>
> Revelation 12:7-9

God did not call a committee meeting to mediate the dispute and decide which of them would be number one. No, the devil was cast out of heaven, no ifs, ands, or buts. However, notice that the anointing is convincing. With what God had given him, Lucifer convinced a great multitude of angels that he was right to exalt himself. He convinced them that he would succeed in his plan, and their agreement cost them their place in heaven as well.

Can you imagine what God went through? Here was one of His prized creations coming against Him — a created being trying to make himself equal to the Creator! Lucifer used the power and anointing God gave him to convince those about him in the angelic realm that he was as great as God. That was a real public relations campaign! They were so thoroughly convinced that they fought for Lucifer against Michael and all the other angels who stayed loyal to God.

Lucifer and his crowd lost that day. They lost their positions and their anointings — they lost it all. Now they hate God and everyone who serves Him. So if you have made Jesus Lord of your life, welcome to boot camp! You are in the army of God. You can expect the enemy to come against you. He will do everything in his power to stop you from living for God and from being effective for the kingdom of God. But Jesus provided the victory for us! We just have to learn how to war a good warfare.

The Lord knoweth how to deliver the godly out of temptations, and to reserve the unjust unto the day of judgment to be punished.

2 Peter 2:9

Nay, in all these things we are more than conquerors through him that loved us.

For I am persuaded, that neither death, nor life, nor angels, nor principalities, nor powers, nor things present, nor things to come,

Nor height, nor depth, nor any other creature, shall be able to separate us from the love of God, which is in Christ Jesus our Lord.

Romans 8:37-39

Chapter 4

Why the Mighty
Heroes Have Fallen

In the 1980s, some mighty heroes of faith fell flat on their faces. Many people backslid because of their shock and disappointment in man. Of course, Christians should not lean on man or rely on other men for their spiritual stability because men are fallible. However, people should be able to trust spiritual leaders, who have a responsibility to the Lord and their followers.

JOSEPH'S SOURCE OF STRENGTH

I sought the Lord as to why preachers fall to temptation. The answer He gave me is the same reason why men of God fell in Bible days. For example, Joseph and Samson were men of God with mighty anointings. Both had profound effects on their generations. Both were used by God. Both faced the same temptation. Both had the same opportunity to fall. One fell, and one did not.

We will see that one had two sources of strength, and the other only had one source.

> Now Israel loved Joseph more than all his children, because he was the son of his old age: and he made him a coat of many colours.
>
> And when his brethren saw that their father loved him more than all his brethren, they hated him, and could not speak peaceably unto him.
>
> And Joseph dreamed a dream, and he told it his brethren: and they hated him yet the more.
>
> **Genesis 37:3-5**

Joseph was in a very interesting position. His earthly father bestowed more favor upon him than on his eleven brothers, even though he was not the firstborn. His brothers resented this special treatment, but when God also began to use Joseph more than them, they developed a murderous hatred. Instead of killing Joseph, however, they sold him as a slave to a caravan of Ishmaelites on their way to Egypt. There, he was resold to Potiphar, Pharaoh's captain of the guard. (See Genesis 37:26-36.)

> And the Lord was with Joseph, and he was a prosperous man; and he was in the house of his master the Egyptian.
>
> And his master saw that the Lord was with him, and that the Lord made all that he did to prosper in his hand.
>
> And Joseph found grace in his sight, and he served him: and he made him overseer over his house, and all that he had he put into his hand.

And it came to pass from the time that he had made him overseer in his house, and over all that he had, that the Lord blessed the Egyptian's house for Joseph's sake; and the blessing of the Lord was upon all that he had in the house, and in the field.

And he left all that he had in Joseph's hand; and he knew not aught he had, save the bread which he did eat. And Joseph was a goodly person, and well favoured.

Genesis 39:2-6

God was with Joseph, and everything he put his hand to prospered. The anointing of God was upon him. He was also good-looking and possessed inner strength. In spite of his circumstances, his character was solid.

Think about Joseph's situation for a minute. His own brothers sold him into slavery! It would be easy for anyone in his position to have a real attitude problem, to wallow in self-pity and rage with resentment, but he did not yield to those things. He did the best he could for his master while never losing sight of the dream God had given him. Because Joseph made the best of a difficult situation, God blessed him and his master.

And it came to pass after these things, that his master's wife cast her eyes upon Joseph; and she said, Lie with me.

But he refused, and said unto his master's wife, Behold, my master wotteth not (does not have to think about) what is with me in the house, and he hath committed all that he hath to my hand;

There is none greater in this house than I; neither hath he kept back any thing from me but thee, because thou art his wife: how then can I do this great wickedness, and sin against God?

And it came to pass, as she spake to Joseph day by day, that he hearkened not unto her, to lie by her, or to be with her.

Genesis 39:7-10 (author's insert)

This is a graphic demonstration of Joseph's inner strength. He said, "No!" immediately when his master's wife propositioned him. Although she kept trying to seduce him day after day, he kept refusing. He continued to stand on his godly principles.

A LACK OF DISCIPLINE

We can contrast Joseph's actions with Samson's.

Then went Samson to Gaza, and saw there an harlot, and went in unto her.

Judges 16:1

Samson exercised no resistance at all. He saw the prostitute and immediately went to her. There was no restraint. *I want her, and I want her now* were his only thoughts. He did not know how to say, "No," to his soul or his body. Discipline was missing from his life.

Still another woman was to become the object of his desire.

And it came to pass afterward, that he loved a woman in the valley of Sorek, whose name was Delilah.

And the lords of the Philistines came up unto her, and said unto her, Entice him, and see wherein his great strength lieth, and by what means we may prevail against him, that we may bind him to afflict him: and we will give thee every one of us eleven hundred pieces of silver.

Judges 16:4-5

Samson had been terrorizing the Philistine oppressors. Under God's anointing, he had single-handedly killed more than a thousand of them. (See Judges 15:15-16.) He carried off the gates of Gaza while the men in the city were waiting in ambush to kill him. The only weakness they could find in Samson was his lack of self-control where women were concerned. No other weapon was effective against him.

Delilah readily accepted the proposition of the Philistine leaders and used all her wiles to get Samson to tell her the secret of his great strength. But instead of immediately refusing to reveal the secret of his power, Samson toyed with Delilah, lying to her three times about how his strength could be neutralized. Each time, the Philistines were waiting to pounce on him, and each time he jumped up and whipped them.

Samson must have been pretty dense not to have seen the pattern. His lust for the woman blinded him to what basic common sense would have shown him. He did not deal with the issue; he played with it.

And it came to pass, when she pressed him daily
with her words, and urged him, so that his soul was
vexed unto death;

That he told her all his heart.

Judges 16:16-17

Samson, who had an anointing that could paralyze the
enemy by the hundreds, fell right down in the lap of a nagging
Delilah and lost everything. No one else in the recorded history
of Israel was anointed with the incredible physical strength
manifested through Samson, yet he lost it all through the lust
of the flesh.

**And she made him sleep upon her knees; and she
called for a man, and she caused him to shave off the
seven locks of his head; and she began to afflict him,
and his strength went from him.**

**And she said, The Philistines be upon thee, Samson.
And he awoke out of his sleep, and said, I will go out
as at other times before, and shake myself. And he wist
not that the Lord was departed from him.**

Judges 16:19-20

Everyone faces a "Delilah" in life. Delilah is not always a
woman or sex problems. Delilah may be money, power, or
possessions — anything that causes one to turn away from
God's will for them. Delilah is lust, a consuming desire for
something not of God. It is uncontrolled wants and causes a
short circuit in our spiritual life. When we fall prey to things

that are not of God, we are not operating by the power of His Holy Spirit and we are forsaking His wisdom. The sad thing is that Samson had access to God's wisdom, but he didn't use it. Do not be like Samson. God's wisdom and power are there for you to stand against the enemy and everything he throws at you.

Happy is the man that findeth wisdom, and the man that getteth understanding.

For the merchandise of it is better than the merchandise of silver, and the gain thereof than fine gold.

She is more precious than rubies: and all the things thou canst desire are not to be compared unto her.

Length of days is in her right hand; and in her left hand riches and honour.

Her ways are ways of pleasantness, and all her paths are peace.

She is a tree of life to them that lay hold upon her: and happy is every one that retaineth her.

Proverbs 3:13-18

WHAT WAS THE DIFFERENCE?

Why was Joseph able to resist when Samson could not? The temptation was the same. What factor made the difference? Why do some call upon the strength and wisdom of the Lord and others do not? Why do the anointed fall?

My grandparents were Assemblies of God ministers, and they told me story after story about how they used to travel and start churches in North and South Carolina. One story in particular really bugged me. There was a minister with such a powerful anointing that all he had to do was raise his hand and everyone in the prayer line would be slain in the Spirit at once. Many healings took place. Yet he ran off with one of the women in the church and divorced his wife. It really bothered me that something like that could happen.

I have studied some of the great men and women of God, and what I have seen troubles me. How could John Alexander Dowie build a great city and be one of the greatest apostles of healing, yet die an invalid, believing he was Elijah?

In 1908, the great Azusa Street Revival waned because of a combination of strife among the brethren and spiritism.

In 1955, miracle revivalist A. A. Allen was arrested for drunken driving.

In 1960, William Branham, a great prophet of God, began to teach heresy.

In 1987 and 1988, two televangelists — Jim Bakker and Jimmy Swaggert — fell in moral scandals.

How could these things happen? Did they love God with all their hearts? I believe the answer is yes. Did God really call them to preach the Gospel? Again, I believe the answer is yes. Then what happened to them that allowed sin and error to overtake their lives and ministries?

I cried out to the Lord and studied the people of the Bible, and I believe the Lord has shown me one of the reasons these things are possible. The anointing is not meant for our practical, everyday living. Strength of character, the authority of the inner man — the human spirit — gives us the ability to resist temptation and do what is right every day. The anointing does not help you resist sin.

Joseph's inner man was strong. His spirit was in charge, so he did not waver when temptation came. On the other hand, Samson's soul and body overpowered his spirit, causing him to yield immediately when he saw the prostitute. Joseph had the anointing *and* a strong inner man; Samson only had the anointing. Without a strong spirit, the soul and body of man will run wild, bringing about destruction.

The anointing is for public service, not private life. Many people try to live off the anointing and fail to allow their spirits to be strong and fervent. A person with a weak inner man will not be able to take authority over his soul or body, and when the anointing lifts and temptation comes, he will fall as Samson did.

I began to find out that the key is not how anointed you are that counts; it is how strong you are in your inner man behind closed doors. Do you really know God and have that close, intimate relationship with Him in private, or do you only know the anointing for public service? Are you a public success and a private failure?

It is easy to live the Christian life when those around you are living that way also. But where life really counts is behind closed doors in the privacy of your home. How do you act then? What kind of witness are you in front of your spouse and your children?

I know ministers who are like Dr. Jekyll and Mr. Hyde. They have two personalities instead of one. Behind the pulpit, they are loving, strong, and bold, but at home they have no strength, no joy, and no love. Their personal relationship with the Lord is weak, and when all their fleshly efforts fail, they get depressed and go through great turmoil.

A minister's wife came to me after I preached on this subject and said, "When I married my husband, he was the same man in both worlds — in public and at home — but now he's like two different people. When he comes home, he's always depressed and worn out. He doesn't want to do anything but sit there and stare into outer space. He's doing things that aren't right, but I don't know what to do about it."

I said, "Play the tape of this sermon (one I had preached on this same subject) a lot around him. Encourage him to pray in tongues and pray with him. Pray fervently, and begin to help him redevelop his inner man and put the Word inside him. Also, give him time to allow his physical body to regain its strength."

Many people say, "Well, I've prayed and nothing happened," but they do not pray the right way. When they get behind closed doors, they pray weak prayers without authority, or they complain and gripe rather than pray. God doesn't want to hear us complaining, He wants us to speak His Word over the situation. You have to stay in the Word and pray the Word with authority to build your inner man if you are going to be like Joseph instead of Samson. It is not a one-shot deal; it is an everyday procedure. Build your inner man and keep your spirit strong.

When I first began in the ministry, I used to say, "If I could live behind the pulpit — if I could sleep, eat, and do everything there — I'd have the most wonderful life." I said that because when I was in the pulpit, I felt secure and protected. But when I stepped out into the world, tremendous opposition would come against me. I did not like that. Finally, God said to me, "Why can't you have Me in the hotel room as strong as you have Me in the pulpit?"

I said, "Well, You know, why not?"

That is when He began to teach me: "You have to build your inner man. Your spirit must be strengthened."

I believe your spirit should be stronger than your anointing. Then there will be more joy in your ministry and work, and your life will not be a constant roller-coaster ride. All that up-and-down business that causes confusion in your life will fade away in the peace of God that comes from a strong inner man.

BUILDING THE HUMAN SPIRIT

Blessed is the man that endureth temptation: for when he is tried, he shall receive the crown of life, which the Lord hath promised to them that love him.

> Let no man say when he is tempted, I am tempted of
> God: for God cannot be tempted with evil, neither
> tempteth he any man:
>
> But every man is tempted, when he is drawn away of
> his own lust, and enticed.
>
> Then when lust hath conceived, it bringeth forth sin:
> and sin, when it is finished, bringeth forth death.
>
> James 1:12-15

The Word does not say, "Blessed is the man who avoids testing, does not deal with temptation, or runs from trials." We are blessed when we endure temptation. We are to persevere under trials. Enduring and persevering mean we go through that test or trial knowing we are going to come out on the other side victoriously.

The Lord does not want us to run away from what we have to deal with because whatever we run away from will one day own us. Some people want to go over the mountain. Some want to go under it. Others want to go around it. But God has called us to go *through* it. Too many people today do not want to go through anything. They are always looking for the easy way out, which is why they cannot overcome temptation. Their souls and bodies are so undisciplined that their spirits are never able to take charge of anything. Then when temptation comes, they fall like Samson because they do not have what is necessary to resist.

If you want to be like Joseph and not like Samson, there are certain principles you need to live by. You need to build these principles on the inside of you and keep them established, so you can live the way God wants you to live every day. They will bring you stability and get you off the roller coaster, where one minute you are ready to take on the whole world and the next minute you can hardly get up and breathe.

The apostle Paul prayed that Jesus **would grant you, according to the riches of his glory, to be strengthened with might by his Spirit in the inner man** (Ephesians 3:16). Paul knew the value of having a strong inner man. The strength of his spirit helped him go through one trial after another and come out victorious and unwavering. (See 2 Corinthians 11:23-31.)

You build up the human spirit by staying in the Word, praying fervently, surrendering everything to God, and keeping the correct associations.

STAYING IN THE WORD

Your physical body needs food regularly to maintain its strength, and so does your spirit. The inner man feeds on the Word of God. Dr. Kenneth E. Hagin often says that too many Christians feed their bodies three square meals a day but only give their spirits one cold snack a week. Your spirit needs a daily diet of the Word to grow strong and bear fruit.

But he that received seed into the good ground is he that heareth the word, and understandeth it; which also beareth fruit, and bringeth forth, some an hundredfold, some sixty, some thirty.

Matthew 13:23

But the fruit of the Spirit is love, joy, peace, longsuffering, gentleness, goodness, faith,

Meekness, temperance: against such there is no law.

And they that are Christ's have crucified the flesh with the affections and lusts.

If we live in the Spirit, let us also walk in the Spirit.

Galatians 5:22-25

Consistently sowing God's Word into your inner man will make your spirit stronger. The stronger your inner man becomes, the more fruit you will see in your life. Walking in the Spirit means you have crucified the flesh. You have taken full authority over your soul and body. Every part of your being is in submission to Jesus Christ, and bearing fruit is a way of life, not an occasional happening. The proper alignment of spirit, soul, and body is of great importance for building a strong inner man.

Staying in the Word also brings freedom and prosperity.

Then said Jesus to those Jews which believed on him, If ye continue in my word, then are ye my disciples indeed;

And ye shall know the truth, and the truth shall make you free.

John 8:31-32

This book of the law shall not depart out of thy mouth; but thou shalt meditate therein day and night, that thou mayest observe to do according to all that is written therein: for then thou shalt make thy way prosperous, and then thou shalt have good success.

Joshua 1:8

This last scripture is the instruction God gave to Joshua as he led the children of Israel into the Promised Land. Staying in the Word builds the inner man so we can bear good fruit and walk in freedom, prosperity, and success. Without the Word, the inner man becomes weaker and weaker, yielding a fruitless life of bondage, poverty, and failure. The choice is ours.

PRAYING FERVENTLY

The effectual fervent prayer of a righteous man availeth much.

James 5:16

How fervent are your prayers? Are you praying with an unmatched passion? Is there a burning desire within you to enter God's presence and hear His voice? A fervent prayer is intense and involved. It means your spirit, soul, and body are all involved. When you pray, is your mind with you or is it in another world? Is your body disciplined, or is it wanting to lie down and go to sleep? If your soul and body are split, you cannot pray fervently. Your house is divided against itself.

And if a house be divided against itself, that house cannot stand.

Mark 3:25

You cannot pray with boldness, intensity, and authority until you get your mind, emotions, and body under the control of your spirit. You need to press into the kingdom of God when you pray. Do not let yourself be concerned over other things during prayer. That is not the time to make out your grocery list or plan your day's activities. Your time of prayer is communion with your heavenly Father and is not to be shared with anything else.

SURRENDERING EVERYTHING TO GOD

I beseech you therefore, brethren, by the mercies of God, that ye present your bodies a living sacrifice, holy, acceptable unto God, which is your reasonable service.

And be not conformed to this world: but be ye transformed by the renewing of your mind, that ye may prove what is that good, and acceptable, and perfect, will of God.

Romans 12:1-2

Verily, verily, I say unto you, Except a corn of wheat fall into the ground and die, it abideth alone: but if it die, it bringeth forth much fruit.

John 12:24

When I went through what I call my six years of training in my bedroom Bible school, I said, "God, is there anything left that You're going to let me keep? What else do You want, Lord? I've given You everything."

The Lord said, "I want everything you are."

There is a twofold dying involved here. There is a death in just giving your life over to the Lord, and there is a death in getting everything right in your spiritual walk. I believe the second one is more difficult than the first.

Everything you hold on to, God will remove. I would hold on to something, and the next afternoon it would leave. The Lord said, "You will get to the place where it is just Me and you. And you will let Me direct the occurrences of your life and the righteousness of your life."

"But Lord, it's hard and it hurts."

He said, "Didn't you die?"

"But, Lord, I'm still living."

"That's why I'm still clipping," He said.

> **I am the true vine, and My Father is the vinedresser.**
> **Every branch in Me that does not bear fruit, He takes away; and every branch that bears fruit, He prunes it, that it may bear more fruit.**
>
> **John 15:1-2** NASB

Your inner man gets stronger as you surrender everything to God and allow Him to prune away the things that sap your strength. Jesus is the Vine, and the more you surrender to Him and abide in Him, the more His strength flows into you. Unsurrendered areas in your life block the flow of His power and make you unfruitful.

Abide in Me, and I in you. As a branch cannot bear fruit of itself, unless it abides in the vine, so neither can you, unless you abide in Me.

I am the vine, you are the branches; he who abides in Me, and I in him, he bears much fruit; for apart from Me you can do nothing.

If anyone does not abide in Me, he is thrown away as a branch, and dries up; and they gather them, and cast them into the fire, and they are burned.

If you abide in Me, and My words abide in you, ask whatever you wish, and it shall be done for you.

By this is My Father glorified, that you bear much fruit, and so prove to be My disciples.

John 15:4-8 NASB

If you are acting independently of God in any area of your life, you are not abiding in the Vine in that area. Even if it appears to be a good work or a righteous thing, if it is independent of God and unsurrendered to Him, it is of no value. It is unfruitful and needs to be pruned.

As you surrender to God in your spirit, soul, and body, your inner man will be strengthened with might so you can immediately say, "No!" when temptation comes and keep on saying it just like Joseph did. Nothing we want to hang on to in this world is really of any value anyway.

The apostle Paul said nothing was of any value compared with knowing Jesus as Lord.

But what things were gain to me, those I counted loss for Christ.

Yea doubtless, and I count all things but loss for the excellency of the knowledge of Christ Jesus my Lord: for whom I have suffered the loss of all things, and do count them but dung, that I may win Christ,

And be found in him, not having mine own righteousness, which is of the law, but that which is through the faith of Christ, the righteousness which is of God by faith:

That I may know him, and the power of his resurrection, and the fellowship of his sufferings, being made conformable unto his death;

If by any means I might attain unto the resurrection of the dead.

Philippians 3:7-11

God cannot resurrect something that is not dead. Surrender everything to Him and abide in Him. Then He can resurrect those areas in the right way, and if He does not resurrect certain things, you do not need them. Just let them go and go on with God.

ASSOCIATING WITH GODLY PEOPLE

The people around you can have a strong effect on your inner man. Surround yourself with godly men and women, people who are submitted to God. You need to be with those of like, or stronger, spirits, not with those whose souls or bodies are in control.

If you spend all your time with weak, carnal Christians, you may find yourself getting weaker and weaker. I am not telling you to avoid weak Christians, but make sure you have quality time with people who will help you grow spiritually.

Remember: The power to overcome temptation is not found in the anointing — it is found in the building up and development of the human spirit. It is found in keeping the soul and body in line with the spirit. Discouragement will not win over you when you are strong in your inner man. Doubts and fears will not manipulate you and control your life when you are strong in the spirit. You will just laugh at them.

You can be like Smith Wigglesworth who said, "I'm a thousand times bigger on the inside than I am on the outside!"

CHAPTER 5

How to Stir Up
the Gifts of God

Now there are varieties of gifts, but the same Spirit.

And there are varieties of ministries, and the same Lord.

And there are varieties of effects, but the same God who works all things in all persons.

But to each one is given the manifestation of the Spirit for the common good.

1 Corinthians 12:4-7 NASB

If you are a believer, you have a gift of God within you. Every believer does. The gift might not be a pulpit ministry, or even a ministry of helps, but you have a special gift God has placed in you. You may say, "I don't know of any gift I have." Many gifts of God are dormant because people do not recognize them or do not know how to get them to flow through their lives. Christians need to learn to enjoy the gifts God has given them and begin to operate in those gifts.

> **For this reason I remind you to fan into flame the gift of God, which is in you through the laying on of my hands.**
>
> 2 Timothy 1:6 NIV

The apostle Paul was reminding his young pastor friend, Timothy, to stir up the gift of God. That's not something we ask God to do — that is what we are to do. The gifts do not grow and mature automatically. If you have not been using the gift God has placed in you, it is time to do something about it — fan the flame!

> **These things command and teach.**
>
> **Let no man despise thy youth; but be thou an example of the believers, in word, in conversation, in charity, in spirit, in faith, in purity.**
>
> **Till I come, give attendance to reading, to exhortation, to doctrine.**
>
> **Neglect not the gift that is in thee, which was given thee by prophecy, with the laying on of the hands of the presbytery.**
>
> **Meditate upon these things; give thyself wholly to them; that thy profiting may appear to all.**
>
> **Take heed unto thyself, and unto the doctrine; continue in them: for in doing this thou shalt both save thyself, and them that hear thee.**
>
> 1 Timothy 4:11-16

Paul's words are good advice for any minister, but particularly for a young minister. Notice that he said to command and teach these things. He did not say, "Present them, and if you like them, do something with them." No, to command and teach means that you are an example. Make yourself do it whether you want to or not, then teach the people of the church and command them to do it also.

It takes boldness and confidence in the Lord to *command* instead of *suggest*. Do not let anyone despise you or look down on you with contempt because of your physical age or your spiritual age. You can be twenty years old in the natural and be thirty-five spiritually. Be bold, and do not let your physical age hold you back.

You can also be forty in the natural and only a year old in the spirit. But do not let anyone look down on you for being a year-old believer. Be bold in that year, be strong in it, and be happy in it. There is nothing wrong with being a year old spiritually — unless you have been a Christian for many years. In that case, it is time to grow up!

No matter what your age is, rise up and rejoice in the Lord. Be an example to others. Realize that you have a gift placed inside of you by God. That means there is something in you that needs to come out. Do not look for it in your head because it is not there. It is in your spirit man — the real you. God put something in your spirit, and you need to stir it up and cause it to come forth like a mighty river. It is time to take action.

DO NOT HIDE THE GIFT

For the kingdom of heaven is as a man travelling into a far country, who called his own servants, and delivered unto them his goods.

And unto one he gave five talents, to another two, and to another one; to every man according to his several ability; and straightway took his journey.

Then he that had received the five talents went and traded with the same, and made them other five talents.

And likewise he that had received two, he also gained other two.

But he that had received one went and digged in the earth, and hid his lord's money.

After a long time the lord of those servants cometh, and reckoneth with them.

And so he that had received five talents came and brought other five talents, saying, Lord, thou deliveredst unto me five talents: behold, I have gained beside them five talents more.

His lord said unto him, Well done, thou good and faithful servant: thou hast been faithful over a few things, I will make thee ruler over many things: enter thou into the joy of thy lord.

He also that had received two talents came and said, Lord, thou deliveredst unto me two talents: behold, I have gained two other talents beside them.

His lord said unto him, Well done, good and faithful servant; thou hast been faithful over a few things, I will make thee ruler over many things: enter thou into the joy of thy lord.

Then he which had received the one talent came and said, Lord, I knew thee that thou art an hard man, reaping where thou hast not sown, and gathering where thou hast not strawed:

And I was afraid, and went and hid thy talent in the earth: lo, there thou hast that is thine.

His lord answered and said unto him, Thou wicked and slothful servant, thou knewest that I reap where I sowed not, and gather where I have not strawed:

Thou oughtest therefore to have put my money to the exchangers, and then at my coming I should have received mine own with usury.

Take therefore the talent from him, and give it unto him which hath ten talents.

For unto every one that hath shall be given, and he shall have abundance: but from him that hath not shall be taken away even that which he hath.

And cast ye the unprofitable servant into outer darkness: there shall be weeping and gnashing of teeth.

Matthew 25:14-30

The talents in this parable were gifts of God. Like money, the gifts can be invested and multiplied or wasted. Each man had one or more, according to his abilities. The men who exercised or used their gifts were rewarded with more, and that made their lord joyful. They showed themselves worthy of more. The man who hid his gift and did not use it was a lazy, unprofitable servant, and he lost what little he did have.

FEED YOUR SPIRIT

We all get excited when we receive gifts — especially when those gifts are wrapped in fancy packages. But the packaging is not the exciting part; it is what is *inside* of the package — the real gift. In order to find out what the gift is, we must unwrap the package. Think of yourself as the package hiding the gift of God. We need to unwrap the package, find out what the gift is, and allow that gift to flow out with ease. Let me show you some things that have worked for me and have made a difference in my own life.

I used to listen to certain ministry tapes over and over. At first, the tapes taught me a lot. I enjoyed them and they built me up. I did not want to put them aside, but after a while those tapes left me flat. I thought, *Now what's wrong here? There's nothing wrong with that man or his message, so there must be something wrong with me.*

God said, "You need something with more 'oomph' to it. You've learned all you can from that teaching. Find something that feeds your spirit. Find something that stirs you up, gets you excited, and gets you joyful. Find something like that."

That did not mean I did not like those first preachers anymore. I still love them and love to hear them. But I had to find someone who had something additional to feed my spirit. I needed a change of diet.

Find people who feed you and feed your anointing and calling. Find people who will stretch your spiritual understanding and knowledge. If you want to walk in the power of God, you need to listen to preachers who operate in the power of the Holy Spirit. Stop associating with dead things! When you are no longer being fed, you need to move where there is spiritual food for you.

If you are trying to feed your inner man with weak or dead things, you will be wishy-washy and powerless. You will be afraid to deliver the word of the Lord. You will wonder if you are really hearing God. But if your spirit has been stirred up and fed, you will not wonder. You will know what the word of the Lord is. You will be able to stand up against all the forces of hell and say what is right. You will be as solid as the Rock of Gibraltar.

Associate, visit, and spend time with people who stir you up — people who can get you doing something. Be bold in the power of God. If you want to stay weak, keep associating with dead preachers and dead churches. If you want to get results, get bold.

SPEAK IT FORTH

The gifts of God respond to bold calls.

When you boldly say, "Gift of God that is within me, come forth; stir up like a river; spring up within me in Jesus' name," it will come. But do not do it just one time and wait for something to happen. Keep speaking it and believing it until the gift begins to come forth. Soon you will not be saying, "Come forth." You will be saying, "Let's go!" and that gift will begin to operate.

I walk my bedroom floor and cause the gift that is within me to spring up. I cause the gift to move because I call for it to come forth in Jesus' name. I say, "Gift, you belong to me, and you are mine. God, the Creator of heaven and earth, has given you unto me for the work of the kingdom. And this day, I call you forth. I call you forth to come up out of me. Let the word of the Lord come forth. Let the gifts of God come forth."

I pull at it. I pull inwardly and I pull outwardly by speaking it forth. When you speak, your voice needs to have power behind it. Your words cannot be skinny — they need to be fat and powerful. Wimpy words and a wimpy attitude will not change you.

> Speaking to yourselves in psalms and hymns and spiritual songs, singing and making melody in your heart to the Lord;
>
> Giving thanks always for all things unto God and the Father in the name of our Lord Jesus Christ.
>
> Ephesians 5:19-20

This is a good place to start. Learn to speak to yourself and make yourself obedient to God. You can take control. Your mind is like a spoiled child who has to be corrected very often. Teach it to enjoy the Gospel. Teach it to enjoy singing psalms and hymns, praying in tongues, and giving thanks for all things.

When you are having a miserable day and nothing is going your way, don't let the enemy rob you of your joy. Take your eyes off of your circumstances, look in the mirror, and make yourself smile. Cause yourself to rejoice when there is no rejoicing in you. You may not think there is anything to rejoice about, but there is. God created you, He loves you, and He sent His Son to die for you. That is worth rejoicing about!

When you do not feel like rejoicing, turn to the Scriptures. Make these scriptures your prayer.

> Why art thou cast down, O my soul? and why art thou disquieted within me? hope thou in God: for I shall yet praise him, who is the health of my countenance, and my God.
>
> Psalm 42:11

I will be glad and rejoice in thee: I will sing praise to thy name, O thou most High.

Psalm 9:2

O give thanks unto the Lord; for he is good; for his mercy endureth for ever.

Blessed be the Lord God of Israel for ever and ever. And all the people said, Amen, and praised the Lord.

1 Chronicles 16:34,36

For the Lord is good; his mercy is everlasting; and his truth endureth to all generations.

Psalm 100:5

Nay, in all these things we are more than conquerors through him that loved us.

Romans 8:37

You are a victor! Jesus loves you, and there is nothing you cannot overcome through His name, His blood, His Word, and His Spirit. Lean on His everlasting arms and seek His face continually. Rejoice in the God of your salvation. Do not linger or wait, but continue on the path He has set before you.

Let your soul rejoice. Jump for everlasting joy! Let your heart sing new songs of glory. Let your ears hear the words of the Lord. Let your eyes see into the Spirit realm and your hands feel the power of the moving of the Spirit of the living God.

If you are going to be part of God's invading force, do what God tells you to do with wisdom. When Paul told you to stir up the gifts that means you have to take action. You have to do something — you have to walk by faith. You may not have goose bumps every morning when you wake up. You may not even wake up with the word of the Lord on your lips. You may wake up with words of failure surrounding you. The devil will try to fill you with doubt and depression. He will try to make you doubt what God has told you to do. When the devil starts that business, jump on him with both feet. Preach him a sermon on the gifts and callings of God and make him understand who you are in Christ Jesus. Attack him! If you sit there and listen to him long enough you will die, but if you attack you will drive him out of your life.

DO NOT BE ASHAMED OF YOUR GIFT

Do not be ashamed of what God is doing in your life or what He has called you to do.

When God told me to go into the nations of the earth and preach the Gospel, I didn't know how. I had no money, and I had no contacts but Him. So I kept walking the floor and calling forth the gift.

"I am called, and I shall be successful. I will not go any other way but the way God desires for me to go. No matter what comes my way, I shall overcome because the Greater One lives within me. I heed His voice. No one shall cause me to deviate from the path God has called me to walk. No one shall cause me to be ashamed because I glory in Christ and I obey His voice. I rejoice in the Lord my God, and I shall succeed in Jesus' name."

If you will authoritatively speak His Word every morning, every lunchtime, and every evening, you will see results. God wants people who are bold in His service. I am not ashamed to say that I am called to the fivefold ministry. I am glad I am what I am. I am also glad I am not you, and you should be glad you are not me. Do not try to be me — be yourself.

If you are a psalmist, make music. If you are an usher, usher. If you are a businessman, get down to business and do it joyfully. Do not let the devil try to get you to stop doing business. As soon as you know you are anointed to do business, the devil will come along and try to tell you that you are a preacher. Watch out!

Not everyone is called to the fivefold ministry. Trying to call yourself to an office will cause you as much trouble as not answering a call God has for you. Do what God has called you to do. Don't worry about what other people have been called to do. You have enough to do just obeying God's call on your own life.

You need to protect your gift because there are hindrances that will come against you. The enemy will try to keep you from fulfilling God's call. He will try to destroy the operation of your gift or cause it to be laid aside. You do not need to be weird to be spiritual. God does not bless weirdness, and He does not bless stupidity and laziness. Watch over your gift as though it is a little baby. It is real small, and you have to carry it. You have to care for it and guard it.

You need to say, "Lord, where do You want me to go so I can let my baby gift grow a little? What book do You want me to read?" Do not read everything on the shelf. Use some common sense. Ask the Lord what you need to read in order to change and grow.

When that baby gift is born, you have to take care of it or you will be a bad parent — a bad steward. Remember the parable of the ten talents. Prove yourself faithful in the small things so God will give you much. Do you know why certain great spiritual leaders keep getting greater? It is because they show themselves worthy of more. God watches you to see what you do with His gift.

When the new gift comes, God does not give it to you on a silver platter. He puts it in you, but you need to call it forth and give birth to it. The greater the gift is, the more battles you will go through. As you call your gift forth and begin to see it flow, exercise it. Allow it to keep flowing. I give myself over to the Holy Spirit every time I minister. I want Him to manifest through me, and I want the gift inside of me to flow freely.

Commit yourself to "let go and let God." Feed your spirit man. Boldly speak forth your gift. Protect your gift. Keep your gift flowing, and never be ashamed of what God has called and equipped you to do.

Being confident of this very thing, that he which hath begun a good work in you will perform it until the day of Jesus Christ.

Philippians 1:6

CHAPTER 6

HOW TO BE FERVENT

This man was instructed in the way of the Lord; and being fervent in the spirit, he spake and taught diligently the things of the Lord.

Acts 18:25

Not slothful in business; fervent in spirit; serving the Lord.

Romans 12:11

Confess your faults one to another, and pray one for another, that ye may be healed. The effectual fervent prayer of a righteous man availeth much.

James 5:16

The key word in these three verses is *fervent,* which speaks of authoritative strength. This authoritative strength is not in the flesh, but in the spirit. Most people who read James 5:16 think, *Oh, a righteous man's prayer does a lot of work.* But the little word *fervent* can make as much difference to your prayers being answered as understanding righteousness.

As a traveling minister, I often have people walk up to me and say something like this: "I've been praying three hours a day for a month. I've been praying every way and every confession I know, and it doesn't seem to be working."

Know this: If there is a problem in our prayer lives, it is not God's fault. The problem has to be in us. We need to diagnose it and find a solution. We need to find out what we are doing wrong and correct it.

Some people who tell me they have been praying for hours and have not gotten an answer are lying. They really have not been praying that long. They are trying to be superspiritual to impress someone, instead of just being themselves. I don't know who they think they are impressing, but it certainly isn't God, and He's the one who counts. If praying for hours determined spirituality, then the Pharisees and Sadducees would have been the most spiritual people who ever lived. (See Mark 12:38-40.) God doesn't look at our outward actions; He looks upon our hearts.

Some people who are not getting anywhere in prayer are just plain ignorant. They do not know what the Bible says about prayer, so they do their own thing, but God is not in it. However, there are some people who are not lying, ignorant, or flaky. They really have been seeking God. They really have been praying and not getting an answer. They have been doing everything they know to do, but have not gotten the breakthrough.

They have not gotten the answer they need from heaven, and they want to know why.

A HOUSE DIVIDED

I began to ask, "God, why aren't these people getting an answer?"

It bothered me because I was raised in a home where as soon as we went to God, He said, "What?" And we quickly got an answer. So when I entered the ministry and began hearing more and more about people who had trouble getting hold of God, I thought, *What's the problem?*

As I prayed about it, the Lord took me to James 5:16 and made the word *fervent* stand out to me. Then he took me to this next scripture.

And Jesus knew their thoughts, and said unto them, Every kingdom divided against itself is brought to desolation; and every city or house divided against itself shall not stand.

Matthew 12:25

Individually, you are a kingdom, or a house, and you have three distinct parts — a spirit, a soul, and a body. The spirit is the real you, and the soul and body are tools with which you function in this earth. When your physical body dies, it is discarded and will be replaced by a resurrection body when Jesus returns. But your soul — your mind, will, and emotions — will go with your spirit man when you go to heaven because they are attached. You have to deal with the soul here as well as there.

We are to gird our minds for action. (See 1 Peter 1:13.) In other words, we are to bring our soul under control so we will be ready for action. You are not a mind — you have a mind. There is a big difference.

God's proper order is for the body to be in submission to the soul, for the soul to be in submission to the spirit, and for the whole man — spirit, soul, and body — to be in submission to Him. Sadly, far too many Christians are out of order. They are walking around with uncontrolled souls or bodies that are dictating to or blocking their spirits. A weak inner man cannot control an untamed soul. That was Samson's problem. He could not say no to his soul or his body.

If your three parts are divided, you will fall. If you are trying to pray and your body wants to sleep, you are divided and you are not fervent. To be fervent means to have your spirit, your soul, and your body go together as one into that arena of prayer and worship. There is a level of intensity that can only be reached when your three parts are united and functioning as one. James 5:16 could be paraphrased as "the intense prayer of a righteous man is very effective."

Most of us pray divided. Our bodies want to sleep, or eat, or go do something else. Our minds are jumping from one thing to another. If you allow your body and mind to do these things while you are in prayer, you are divided and not fervent. You have to get your soul and body under the leadership of your spirit to be fervent and avail much.

Sometimes when you start praying, your mind will tell you everything you have not done that day. It might get so strong that you quit praying to go do it. When I began to train my mind to stay with me in prayer, I would write down what it would tell me that I had not done yet. Pretty soon I would have a major list of things to do. But finally I said, "No, mind, you're going to obey me." You have to make your head obey you. Sometimes you have to speak to your head and say, "Head, if you don't agree with me — if you keep fighting me — I am going to pray an extra fifteen minutes in other tongues."

I learned how to pray as a child by watching my mother and grandmother pray. When they hit a certain realm in the Spirit, the power of God would fall in the room. Many people never get into that realm of the Spirit, or they only get there when they are in trouble and need something from God. God wants us to live in that realm. That is what makes the Christian life exciting.

FERVENT PRAYER IS A CHOICE

You will never *feel* like praying fervently. It is a choice you have to make every day. Begin making that choice, and God will meet you there. Choose to grab your soul and body and make them join your spirit in prayer.

Acts 18:25 speaks of a minister who was fervent in spirit. That means he disciplined himself, and when he went out to preach, he preached from his whole being. That is what I try to do when I preach. My head is not thinking, *I need to go home and take care of this and that*, and my body is not saying, "I wish I could sleep." When I get in the pulpit, all three parts of me — spirit, soul, and body — are there to preach and to preach fervently. The power of God flows, and the church gets a full meal as a result.

Too many Christians are only getting appetizers on Sunday because their pastors do not have their spirit, soul, and body all together in the pulpit. Pastors who preach and teach the Word of God with fervency — with a passion — have churches that are doing something for the kingdom of God. Those are the churches that are winning the lost and making disciples for Christ.

Romans 12:11 instructs us to be fervent in spirit. God wants us to pray fervently, preach fervently, and live fervently. When you say something, you should believe it and stand on it with all your spirit, soul, and body. If you will live like that, you will not be so easily deceived or scared. There is strength when your spirit, soul, and body are in agreement.

Some Christians live in fear all the time. As soon as they get away from the presence of strong Christians, their heads pull them back into the arena of fear and away from faith. Not being ruled by their spirit man leaves them weak and vulnerable to attack from spirits of fear. Our struggles are not against flesh and blood, but against spiritual forces. (See Ephesians 6:12.) If we try to fight spiritual forces with our flesh, we will succumb to fear every time. But if our spirit man rises up and takes on these battles that face us in the spirit world, we will overcome them by the authority we have in Jesus Christ, and there will be no room for fear.

Confusion sets in when people do not know what they are going to do next. They look at their three options — the body way, the head way, or the spirit way — trying to decide which is going to rule. Sadly, many sit there in the flesh, get worried and frustrated, and usually end up doing nothing. That is why their decisions never stick. When they make a decision, about three minutes later their heads talk them out of it or their bodies do not want to do it, so they forget about it. They are not fervent, and their divided houses fall. You can only be fervent when you know you are standing on truth — God's truth — which clearly says that your spirit should rule.

And he answering said, Thou shalt love the Lord thy God with all thy heart, and with all thy soul, and with all thy strength, and with all thy mind; and thy neighbour as thyself.

Luke 10:27

God expects us to love Him with all of our being, holding nothing back. He expects us to approach Him in prayer the same way with heart, soul, strength, and mind united.

Your spirit knows that your mind and body have to be in agreement with it to have an effectual prayer. Your spirit will try to pull everything together. But if your flesh outweighs it, or if the flesh can pull harder, your spirit will wear itself out and your prayers will not avail much.

This is why people often waste time when they pray. The entire time they are praying, they cannot wait to finish so they can do something else. They are simply going through the motions. They are not really praying. Prayer becomes a formula rather than a productive part of their lives.

If you are praying because it is the thing to do, that stinks. God does not want your formula — He wants you. He wants you to humble your whole being before Him and pray fervently. He wants you to live like that and work like that. Fervency should be your lifestyle.

If you are going to be a Christian, be one with everything that is in you. Forget about being *religious*. Religion is **having a form of godliness, but denying the power thereof** (2 Timothy 3:5). Religion is disgusting to God. He wants a *relationship* with you, not a bunch of religious barriers and jargon. The Bible says to be either hot or cold, right or wrong, in or out, but not lukewarm. (See Revelation 3:15-16.) Either you are with God, or you are not.

Far too many Christians are religious. They have just enough Christianity mixed in with just enough flesh to stay miserable. That is being lukewarm and is no way to live.

The thief cometh not, but for to steal, and to kill, and to destroy: I am come that they might have life, and that they might have it more abundantly.

John 10:10

Fervent Christians have joy and all the other fruits of the Spirit. It is fun to be fervent because you are totally involved. You are in it all the way. That is the *abundant life*. The devil comes to kill, to steal, and to destroy, and if he can divide you, he has you. A house divided will fall quickly in difficult times. (See Luke 11:17.) But fervent Christians are the ones who are going to last in the difficult days ahead. They are the ones who will be overcomers.

FERVENT PRAYERS GET ANSWERED

You can be sitting there praying in tongues, and your body will say, "I don't want to pray in tongues anymore. I want to pray in English." Soon your flesh is dominating your spiritual activities, instead of your spirit dominating your fleshly desires. No wonder you cannot get results. You can wear yourself out going three hours a day trying to find God.

Do not say, "Well, I'm trying to be a good Christian."

Stop trying and do it! There is no way you can pray fervently and not get an answer from God. It is like when children are playing and they call out, "Mom." The mother knows it is no big deal and just goes on with what she is doing. Then it comes more sharply, "MOM!" She drops everything and immediately responds. What was the difference? The second call was fervent. All three parts — spirit, soul, and body — were calling out at the same time, and Mom knew it.

That is how we need to talk to God. All three parts need to say, "GOD!" It is not out of desperation — it is with intensity. I believe if you pray like that, God will hit you with an answer within an hour or two, sometimes sooner. If you learn to be fervent and consistent, you can say, "God!" and He will say, "What?"

God does not talk to your head; He talks to your spirit — the real you. God speaks to your heart because that is where the spirit man lives. Your head might find out about it a few seconds later, but God is going to speak to the real you first.

FERVENT IN CHURCH

You need to be fervent every time you go to church if you want God's best. If you let your flesh rule, you will not have much fun in church. One time your head will want to be intellectual, and you will sit there criticizing the sermon. Another day your body will get mad at the wooden pews and distract you. Your head can be miles away, and you can still sit there and smile.

You will say, "Well, I never get fed at that church." But you were never at that church! Your physical body was there, but your heart and soul were someplace else. Your spirit, soul, and body need to be united when you are at church, not going three different directions. You will not be able to recognize what the Holy Spirit is doing in a service if you are not united. A glory cloud could roll in and fill the auditorium, and you would not know it if your head was thinking about the job, or your body was worrying about the lines at the cafeteria that afternoon.

Make your body walk through the church door. Make your head come with your spirit through that door. Come in there together. If a spirit of heaviness is trying to weigh you down, get fervent in praise and worship and drive that spirit far from you. Look at what happened when the worshippers came together as one during the days of King Solomon.

> It came even to pass, as the trumpeters and singers were as one, to make one sound to be heard in praising and thanking the Lord; and when they lifted up their voice with the trumpets and cymbals and instruments of musick, and praised the Lord, saying, For he is good; for his mercy endureth for ever: that then the house was filled with a cloud, even the house of the Lord;
>
> So that the priests could not stand to minister by reason of the cloud: for the glory of the Lord had filled the house of God.
>
> 2 Chronicles 5:13-14

I believe the same thing can happen in any church of the living God if the people will come together and fervently praise and worship Him. I believe God's heart is yearning to manifest His presence in a greater way in His Church. But before you can be united with everyone else, you have to get your own being united. Then you need to learn how to hook up with the other people. Both are decisions you have to make every time you go to church. You will not do either one automatically. You have to choose to be in unity. When you set your will to do that, you will learn to flow with what God is doing in the services.

Get fervent in prayer. Get fervent in church. Get fervent in every area of your life, and you will find that God will meet you in new and exciting ways. Learn to jump in there and flow with Him because new things are on the way for you.

Chapter 7

The Lord Is a Warrior

Some people do not like to discuss the devil, but I believe we need to learn about our enemy so we are able to better understand his strategies and wage a better war. Never forget that we are in a war! Many people seem to believe that the supernatural realm is imaginary or that somehow it is not real. What an incredible deception! The world of the spirit is more real than the natural realm.

Satan and his hierarchies are not dumb. They know what they are doing. They know human nature and plan their strategies and attacks accordingly. They study our weaknesses and use them against us. Their goal is our destruction and death.

My parents taught me about one of the devil's greatest areas of attack, particularly against young ministers. They said, "Now, Roberts, listen to us. The devil doesn't really mind that you love God as a young man. He'll fight you a little, but he won't fight you too much now. He'll wait until you get to be well-known, when a lot of people will trust your ministry. He has planned his strategy and will find any weakness in your flesh that has not been dealt with. Then when it will hurt the most, he'll hit you at a weak moment and try to knock you out. Most of the time, he's very successful."

When the devil knocks out a big ministry, he also knocks out thousands of people who trusted that ministry. The repercussions ripple throughout the body of Christ.

I am not saying that if you are not involved in a large ministry the devil won't attack you. You became a minister of the Gospel the day you got saved, and Satan will attack any Christian he can. Every single believer is a threat to him, especially those who are fulfilling the call of God on their lives, so we all need to be aware of the devil's devices.

There are three major "killer weapons of the devil" that have been knocking out ministries for generations. If you are a young minister, watching out for these things could save your ministry and possibly your life.

KILLER NO. 1 – PRIDE

Pride caused Satan's fall from heaven and has destroyed many ministries. It is the biggest ditch found in the supernatural realm. People fall into it by the thousands.

Pride is a secret killer. Very subtly, it sets up its home inside of you — in your heart. It begins to feed you thoughts that at first you may forget or throw out, but it will keep feeding them to you. Yes, pride has a voice and it will talk to you where no one else can hear it. What pride says will seem to be true, but it is a trap.

Pride always speaks when you are at the point of needing encouragement and when you need someone to say you are on the right track. It will come in and say, "Yes, you're doing a wonderful job. Look at what happens when people come to your meetings. Look at what you have accomplished for God."

If you accept those thoughts, the big "I" will start growing in you, then the "I wills" will move you from pride to self-will and rebellion, leaving you primed for a big fall. When you walk in humility, God will promote you. When you step over into pride, God will demote you.

Saul is a good example. When he was humble, God anointed him to be the first king over Israel, but he lost it all because he stepped into pride and disobedience. He did not remain small in his own eyes.

Only by pride cometh contention: but with the well advised is wisdom.

Proverbs 13:10

Pride brings strife. God doesn't want us living in strife with our brothers and sisters in the Lord or with Him. When there is strife among believers, His power and love are cut off and the Gospel will not go forth.

Pride also insulates you from godly counsel. Pride will surround itself with flatterers and "yes men," people who will never rise up and confront it. Pride hates confrontation.

But when his heart was lifted up, and his mind hardened in pride, he was deposed from his kingly throne, and they took his glory from him.

Daniel 5:20

Pride hardens the mind. When pride hardens your mind, you cannot think straight. It causes you to make decisions that bring failure. Pride makes you think you can do something when you are not really ready, then you fall when you try to do it. Pride also makes you think you can do things in your own strength without God.

Strangers have devoured his strength, and he knoweth it not: yea, gray hairs are here and there upon him, yet he knoweth not.

And the pride of Israel testifieth to his face: and they do not return to the Lord their God, nor seek him for all this.

Hosea 7:9-10

Pride produces spiritual decay. When you are suffering from spiritual decay, you are not progressing. Pride stunts your spiritual growth because it says you have arrived and no longer need to work towards maturity. Remember this: With God there is no beginning and there is no end, so there will always be a progression. There will never be a day of saying, "I've got it all together."

> The wicked, through the pride of his countenance, will not seek after God: God is not in all his thoughts.

Psalm 10:4

Pride isolates you from God and causes you to reject the Word of God. (See Jeremiah 43:2.) It brings you into self-deception. (See Jeremiah 49:16.)

> **Pride goeth before destruction, and an haughty spirit before a fall.**

Proverbs 16:18

When the fruit of pride is fully ripened, it brings ruin. It is never satisfied. Pride always wants more, and in the end, if it is not dealt with properly, it will kill you.

Three things will help you avoid pride:

• *Remember where you were when God found you.* You will stay humble when you remember where you came from and where God has brought you. You did not bring yourself there — God brought you.

• *Do not believe your own press reports.* People may start "tooting your horn" when you move out in ministry, but do not believe it. Instead, believe God's report that you are a humble servant who is happy because you are obeying God. Your obedience to God is why everything is working right, not because of anything you've done on your own.

• *Stay close to God and give Him all the glory.* That takes a conscious effort. It cannot be done subconsciously. Make the effort! It is impossible to stay close to God and be filled with pride. God is too big, and you cannot compete with Him. Staying close to Him will keep you humble.

Pride is not something you can be delivered of by someone laying hands on you and saying, "Come out." It is a daily fight. For some people, it is a moment-by-moment fight. Make the effort. Do not let pride destroy your ministry or your life.

KILLER NO. 2 – MONEY

We all need money to function in the world, but it is often overrated. Money is a tool of exchange for you to use, but it is not your life. God wants us to prosper, but do not confuse how much money you have with who you are.

Three problem areas can turn money into a killer — greed, debt, and the love of money.

Greed is where you have to have more and more — and still it is not enough. Greed will not allow you to give, but causes you to clutch every cent and never let go. It is all right to have increase. It is all right to have money in the bank and to have a retirement account. But do not allow the spirit of greed to operate in your life. Like pride, greed can never be satisfied because it never has enough. We can avoid greed if we have God's attitude about money, develop a giving heart, and give as the Holy Spirit leads.

But remember the Lord your God, for it is he who gives you the ability to produce wealth.

Deuteronomy 8:18 NIV

God loves a cheerful giver.

2 Corinthians 9:7 NIV

Concerning debt, there is a great debate about whether Christians should borrow money or not. I personally believe it is okay to take out loans, but go only as far as your faith and your good conscience will allow you to go. Do not put yourself into debt to the point where it becomes a weight or a burden on you, and what you owe monopolizes your thinking. Confusion and fear should have no place in your finances.

But they that will be rich fall into temptation and a snare, and into many foolish and hurtful lusts, which drown men in destruction and perdition.

For the love of money is the root of all evil: which while some coveted after, they have erred from the faith, and pierced themselves through with many sorrows.

1 Timothy 6:9-10

Money is not the root of evil; the *love* of money is the root of all evil. It is your attitude toward money that is important. Money does not own me — I own it. God can bless me because I give, and I like giving. God likes to prosper His people whose hearts are right. If you find yourself lusting after money — really craving it — it is time to get your attitude adjusted before it kills you. That attitude is idolatry. Do not put money ahead of God.

Money is often a killer in the ministry world because so many ministers have come out of poverty. Their families did not have much money when they were growing up. Then when their ministries grow and the money starts to come in, they do not know how to handle it. They step out of the Spirit and into the flesh, and that opens the door for the enemy to turn their blessings into cursings.

Staying close to Jesus will help you keep your heart right and your attitude straight. Keeping Jesus first makes the other areas of your life find their proper place.

Moreover, when God gives any man wealth and possessions, and enables him to enjoy them, to accept his lot and be happy in his work — this is a gift of God.

He seldom reflects on the days of his life, because God keeps him occupied with gladness of heart.

Ecclesiastes 5:19-20 NIV

KILLER NO. 3 – SEX

Financial sins are sins that come because of money. They have a short life compared to the problems that result from sexual sins. Sexual sins live. They will haunt you because sex is the only act that involves the creation of another soul. It is not what you might call a small, quiet sin! Sexual sin will directly affect another person's life, and indirectly, it can affect many lives. Sadly, many sexual sins involve abortion — murder.

The devil plays on a God-given physical drive and orchestrates events to put you into a position where he can push your button. If you yield when he pushes your button, he has knocked you out. If you do not know how to hold the reins on your sexual drive, it will haunt you and could eventually destroy you.

Every time you start to move forward, the enemy will say, "Remember what you did? Remember how guilty you felt afterwards?" He wants to beat you up with the memory of what he pushed you to do in the first place.

There is only one way to avoid all of this — get in the glory of God and stay there. Stay high in His presence. If you have sinned in this way, understand that you can receive forgiveness. However, if you created an "Ishmael," you are responsible for it. The consequences of the sin may not go away when forgiveness comes. Forgiveness from God wipes out the sin but does not always wipe out the consequences.

If you are not married, do not allow your emotional or physical needs to fool you into thinking you love the wrong person. Wait until you know from God the one you are dating is the right one. Do not go by what you think or feel. Find out from God. Participating in soulish love sets you up for hurt when the relationship breaks up — or worse, marriage to the wrong person and perhaps divorce. Stay in God's agape love. Keep the reins on your flesh until God says, "Yes, this is the one," and you walk down that aisle and make the marriage vow to one another.

If you are married, keep the lines of communication open at all times. If a problem arises, go to your spouse and both of you go to God. Work it out together. Decide together what you are going to do about the problem. Staying in agreement leaves no room for the spirit of strife and contention to enter.

Men, avoid the trap of talking about your problems with your secretary or your female co-workers. Women likewise, do not take your problems to a friend of the opposite sex. That could create an emotional intimacy that might open the door to physical intimacy.

Pastors, you should not be counseling a member of the opposite sex alone. Your spouse should sit in with you. Do not create opportunities for sexual sin to enter. Build resisters inside yourself. Put chapter and verse against temptation in your heart in order to be able to say to the devil, **It is written** (Matthew 4:7). If your mind begins to wander, direct it back where it belongs.

> **Casting down imaginations, and every high thing that exalteth itself against the knowledge of God, and bringing into captivity every thought to the obedience of Christ.**
>
> **2 Corinthians 10:5**

Finally, brethren, whatsoever things are true, whatsoever things are honest, whatsoever things are just, whatsoever things are pure, whatsoever things are lovely, whatsoever things are of good report; if there be any virtue, and if there by any praise, think on these things.

Philippians 4:8

Sometimes you have to speak boldly to yourself. Say, "No, mind, you cannot think that way. I own you, and I will not allow you to play with ideas like that." If you do not talk to yourself, the devil will. Otherwise, you may wake up some morning and say, "Why did I do that?" But then it will be too late.

Know the devices of the devil and fight them. Particularly be aware of the three killers I have mentioned — pride, money, and sex. Great ministers have fallen at the height of their greatest potential for God because of these killers. It does not take two or three times. Once can stop your ministry for a lifetime.

LET THE DEVIL KNOW WHO YOU ARE

Finally, my brethren, be strong in the Lord, and in the power of his might.

Put on the whole armour of God, that ye may be able to stand against the wiles of the devil.

For we wrestle not against flesh and blood, but against principalities, against powers, against the rulers of the darkness of this world, against spiritual wickedness in high places.

Ephesians 6:10-12

Every person who obeys God is going to confront demons — not once, but many times — but never forget that the Greater One lives inside you. (See 1 John 4:4.) You are a victor through Jesus Christ. (See Romans 8:37.) You are more than a conqueror, so let the devil know it by hitting him with the power Jesus has delegated to you through His name.

Quit being nice to the devil! Get him out of your house and off your street. Do not let him give you a headache — give him one! Use the sword of the Spirit as the offensive weapon that it is. Make him worry about where you are going to hurt his kingdom next. He should be defending against your attacks instead of you defending against his. Be part of God's invading force.

When you go to war, you do not go alone. God dispatches His angels to fight with you. (See Hebrews 1:14.) When you step out in obedience to God, you hook up with all the other warriors of the kingdom.

If you are walking in faith and being led by the Holy Spirit, the Lord will show you things to come. He will show you what kind of an attack the devil is going to try to mount against your home. The devil will try to tear up your marriage and destroy your children, but when you know what the plan is, you can take the battle into his territory and defeat him before he ever gets a chance to bring the battle into your home. If the battle is already in your home, you will have to drive him out, then fortify your territory to keep him from coming back.

One of the biggest secrets to having a happy home is being in tune with God and taking the battle to the devil's territory in the spiritual realm. The man of the house needs to learn that being on his knees before the Lord is a position of manhood. The whole family needs to band together in spiritual warfare, but the man should take the most responsibility. If you are a single mother, then the responsibility to do battle for your family rests on you. Don't use the excuse that you're not married. Through the power of the Holy Spirit you can smack the devil in the face as well as any man!

THE REALITY OF WARFARE

The Lord burned a picture of the reality of warfare into my mind when He sent me to Africa. We were not playing cowboys and Indians — it was real. The Lord sent us to a little Assemblies of God church in Zobo, a city in the communist nation of Mozambique. He sent me to teach them how to fight demons.

Mozambique was in a state of civil war with rebels fighting against the nation's communist troops. We traveled as part of a Zimbabwe army convoy that had to cross Mozambique to carry supplies between Zimbabwe and Malawi. We headed for Zobo right through some of the areas where the heaviest fighting was taking place.

I thought, *If anything is going to happen, it will happen on the way over to Zobo.* I sat in front of the truck to watch and pray. Praise God, nothing happened. I preached that night, and early the next morning we caught the convoy back. I got in the back of the truck this time so I could lie down and sleep. At about 6:35 a.m., gunfire started. I was an American teenager at the time who knew nothing about guns or gunfire, so I just turned over and went back to sleep.

When the gunfire got closer, someone hit the back of the truck and said, "Get up! Get out!" So I got up, sat on the back of the truck, and looked around.

I turned to my associate, Scott, and said, "This is just like television. Look at this!" That was not one of the most intelligent things I have ever done. I thought the battle was down the road, when in fact we were right in the middle of the crossfire! And our white skin made us stand out like neon signs in the morning light.

When one of the Zimbabwe soldiers was hit and killed, I finally realized we were not in a game or watching a John Wayne movie. We could no longer stay in the middle of the road and be amused by machine gun bullets clipping the bushes.

I got a revelation of the reality of the situation, but we had not been trained in physical warfare. So we just walked over and sat down in the ditch, when we should have run and jumped in the ditch as soon as we left the truck. The Mozambique rebels shooting at the convoy were trying to capture supplies because they were starving.

One of them came up on top of us, and I thought, *Lord, are You there?*

Fear tried to grip my heart. If you allow fear to grip you, you are in big trouble. Never react in the natural; always respond in the Spirit. That is an important key in spiritual warfare. Do not touch it in the natural or with your mind. Let your spirit respond.

I did not have time to pull out a faith tape or remember a formula. If I had tried to remember every faith outline I had heard or preached, I would have died. My spirit responded with Psalm 62:8: **Trust in him at all times; ye people, pour out your heart before him: God is a refuge for us. Selah.**

I had to trust God and allow Him to be my refuge. I could not pick up a gun and fight because I did not know how. Eventually the fighting ceased, and it was only a miracle of God that we were still alive. The rebel disappeared as suddenly as he had appeared.

Our ignorance easily could have cost us our lives, and that is the point of my story. Many people approach spiritual warfare the way I approached that battle in the natural. At first it seems like fun — like a game. It seems unreal until the first time you really take a blow. Do not play games with spiritual warfare. Realize the fight is real. You will be attacked, but if you know the tactics of the enemy you will be better prepared for battle. You will know what is going on and respond instead of wandering around in a daze.

On the way out of that incident, God said, "I wanted you to see where my Church stands today. I wanted you to experience how My believers stand today. I wanted you to sense the fear, to see the torture, to see the death that happens in the world of the spirit for those who do not know how to fight the devil. What you saw in the natural is what happens in the spiritual realm every single day on earth. I see them die. I see them shot. I see them out there playing games, not taking it seriously. My kingdom suffers. My people are lost because they are not seeing reality. They think it is a game. It is imaginary to some.

"But I want you to know that the battle we are in is real. People suffer. People die spiritually because you do not pray and you do not fight. It is real out here in the spiritual realm. The talk of being in a war is true. It is not a figure of speech."

OBEDIENCE THREATENS THE ENEMY

The closer you walk with God, the greater understanding of spiritual battles you will have. When you obey God in the world of the spirit, you threaten and harm the powers of the devil. A Christian in the natural does not threaten the devil like an obedient believer does in the spirit world, because Satan's ultimate plan is to destroy the Gospel, and obedient believers are advancing the Gospel.

When you really step out into that spiritual realm, you become a big target for the devil because you can hurt him. Nearly everywhere you go you will find yourself in a battle. I travel at least twenty days out of the month and go from one battle to another.

Far too many churches have no awareness of the battle that takes place in the spiritual realm, so demons have free reign over them. I have to fight a battle just to get into the pulpit and preach in some places. The glory is a weapon too. You can pray until the glory falls, and it will scare the devil out of the place.

We have to fight the good fight of faith, and that fight is not in the natural. We do not fight against other people. We battle principalities and powers and wicked spirits in heavenly places. (See Ephesians 6:12.)

PICK UP THE WEAPONS

Be strong in the power of His might and pick up the weapons God has given you. Make Him glad you are a member of His army. When you accept Jesus as your personal Savior, you go into boot camp. When you learn the lessons of boot camp, you go to war. Then there are those who go into special training. Their goal is to become the Green Berets of the Spirit.

Instead of walking around and sowing strife, the Green Berets of the Spirit sow truth. They encourage people in the faith. Soon there is no discord when people get together. They start shouting and praying, the glory falls, and the devil has lost again.

The prophets of God are coming like spies. They go in behind the battle lines and sneak into the enemy's headquarters.

They steal the code books and the strategy books. They return to the Church with those plans and say, "This is what the enemy plans to do, and this is how God says we should stop it."

The Lord recently told me, "I have given the Church many weapons, but they never read the manual on how to use them. That is why they are being shot to death while they are holding the most powerful weapon in the universe in their hands. They don't know how to shoot because they don't read the manual." It is time we learn how to shoot our spiritual guns. It is time we launch demon-seeking missiles in the spirit. It is time to go to battle.

Too many Christians today think they are on vacation, while the world is crumbling all around them. There are no furloughs in God's army, so get into the battle and win! Drive the enemy out of your territory, then go look for new territory to conquer.

PAUL'S EXAMPLE

The apostle Paul fought many spiritual battles.

And it came to pass, as we went to prayer, a certain damsel possessed with a spirit of divination met us, which brought her masters much gain by soothsaying:

The same followed Paul and us, and cried, saying, These men are the servants of the most high God, which shew unto us the way of salvation.

And this did she many days. But Paul, being grieved, turned and said to the spirit, I command thee in the name of Jesus Christ to come out of her. And he came out the same hour.

Acts 16:16-18

Paul did not *react* in the natural — he *responded* in the Spirit. Paul did not come against the woman; he launched his attack against the demon in her and drove it out of her. When you cast out an evil spirit, all the other demons in the vicinity know about it. Be prepared because sometimes they get together and counterattack.

And when her masters saw that the hope of their gains was gone, they caught Paul and Silas, and drew them into the marketplace unto the rulers,

And brought them to the magistrates, saying, These men, being Jews, do exceedingly trouble our city,

And teach customs, which are not lawful for us to receive, neither to observe, being Romans.

And the multitude rose up together against them: and the magistrates rent off their clothes, and commanded to beat them.

And when they had laid many stripes upon them, they cast them into prison, charging the jailer to keep them safely:

Who, having received such a charge, thrust them into the inner prison, and made their feet fast in the stocks.

And at midnight Paul and Silas prayed, and sang praises unto God: and the prisoners heard them.

And suddenly there was a great earthquake, so that the foundations of the prison were shaken: and immediately all the doors were opened, and every one's bands were loosed.

Acts 16:19-26

The demons counterattacked by having the girl's masters stir up the crowds and the local magistrates. Paul and Silas were severely beaten and thrown into the deepest part of the prison, but they did not despair. They were prisoners of war, but they did not stay that way long. They sang and praised God, joyfully continuing the battle, and God supernaturally delivered them.

From the lips of children and infants you have ordained praise because of your enemies, to silence the foe and the avenger.

Psalm 8:2 NIV

If you get captured when you obediently go into spiritual warfare, God will not leave you as a prisoner of war for long. Paul's and Silas's deliverance came when they began to worship God. Our praise to God stills the enemy. Be diligent in your time of daily praise and worship. Stay in the joy and the peace of the Lord, and He will deliver you and take you into victory.

Believe God. Fight the devils. Praise God and enjoy the victory.

The joy of the Lord is your strength.

Nehemiah 8:10

CHAPTER 8

THE POWER OF GODLY CONFRONTATION

The word *confrontation* makes a lot of people nervous — Christians included. When the word is used in the context of fighting devils, it does not bother them, but when confrontation is used in connection with training, personal growth, and correction, they do not like it. People tend to resist change, but God expects us to change.

> **But we all, with open face beholding as in a glass the glory of the Lord, are changed into the same image from glory to glory, even as by the Spirit of the Lord.**
>
> 2 Corinthians 3:18

God's plan is for us to be changed into the image of Jesus Christ. We are to be like Him in spirit, soul, and body. However, our souls and bodies will not change unless they are confronted with the difference between

God's ideal and our current reality. The same thing applies to churches. Change will not come without confrontation.

Confrontation can come in a variety of ways, ranging from a gentle hint to a bold word that hits hard. How it comes, when it comes, and through whom it comes should all be directed by the Holy Spirit.

In recent decades, the body of Christ has replaced godly confrontation with gushy, sloppy, soulish love — a perverted love. If we keep walking in this gushy stuff, we will not prevail and we will not avail much for the kingdom of God.

There is a powerful sweet anointing and a powerful bold anointing. Both are from God. But if you only accept one of them, you will have a problem. If you stay stuck in the sweet, you will never know the bold. If you stay stuck in the bold, you will never know the sweet. You need to know how to flow back and forth between the two as the Spirit leads.

If you are already uncomfortable with this chapter, please do not quit reading now. I have found that the sermons I least like are the ones I need the most. Your mind and emotions fight against them because they don't want to change. They feel anything that brings change is an attack and a threat.

> For the word of God is quick, and powerful, and sharper than any twoedged sword, piercing even to the dividing asunder of soul and spirit, and of the joints and marrow, and is a discerner of the thoughts and intents of the heart.
>
> **Hebrews 4:12**

The Word of God is sharp and powerful. Properly applied, it can set people free. On the other hand, if it is not used properly it can wound and kill. *This is why the person applying the Word must be led by the Spirit.* I cannot emphasize that enough.

Many people have been wounded and hacked to death by soulish Christians wielding the sword of the Word like an ax. That sword needs to be handled as a skillful surgeon uses a scalpel to cut out a cancerous growth, leaving everything around it untouched.

Sometimes ministers see a problem and go after it with all their might. While we are killing it, we are mutilating everything else and there is nothing left when we get through. Some preachers have lost their ministries because they were undisciplined and unskilled surgeons. They operated without the discipline and training of the Spirit, leaving a trail of mutilated people. Eventually they got called on God's carpet for malpractice — for abusing the sheep. The Bible gives us many examples of Spirit-led confrontation we can follow to avoid dishing out death and destruction to our brothers and sisters in the Lord.

JOHN THE BAPTIST

In those days came John the Baptist, preaching in the wilderness of Judaea,

And saying, Repent ye: for the kingdom of heaven is at hand.

For this is he that was spoken of by the prophet
Esaias, saying, The voice of one crying in the wilderness,
Prepare ye the way of the Lord, make his paths straight.

Matthew 3:1-3

How do you prepare the way of the Lord? How do you make
crooked paths straight? You can't just look at them; you have to
confront them. You have to straighten them out. Crooked paths
are those we make to keep our flesh comfortable. We don't want
to have to give up anything as we travel down the spiritual path.

And the same John had his raiment of camel's hair,
and a leathern girdle about his loins; and his meat was
locusts and wild honey.

Then went out to him Jerusalem, and all Judaea, and
all the region round about Jordan,

And were baptized of him in Jordan, confessing
their sins.

But when he saw many of the Pharisees and
Sadducees come to his baptism, he said unto them, O
generation of vipers, who hath warned you to flee from
the wrath to come?

Bring forth therefore fruits meet for repentance:

And think not to say within yourselves, We have
Abraham for our father: for I say unto you, that God is
able of these stones to raise up children unto Abraham.

And now also the ax is laid unto the root of the trees:
therefore every tree which bringeth not forth good fruit
is hewn down, and cast into the fire.

Matthew 3:4-10

John the Baptist was called to confrontation: *Repent and be baptized*. His call was not one that would be naturally accepted by a lot of people today. But it is spiritually acceptable to all those who are hungering and thirsting after righteousness, and to those who want to be changed into the image of Jesus Christ.

Every sermon should be confrontational. Every sermon should challenge you. If you are confronted and hungry to have the Word working in your life, you will be happy. If the sermon confronts a sin in your life, it will make you uncomfortable until you repent and experience the cleansing power of God flowing through you. However, if you do not want correction, confrontation will only anger you.

When I go into a church for the first time, I do not know anything about the congregation. As I start preaching by the leading of the Holy Spirit, I can see how the Word is hitting them by the way they react. I hope for happy faces, but in a lot of churches I see straight faces, sad faces, or angry eyebrows. I keep trying to tell them I am a nice guy, but they do not like me when I hit a pet flesh area they are in agreement with.

If ministers do not keep putting the Word out to confront sin, weakness, and wrong, the people will never grow up and be changed into Jesus' image. We have too many congregations today who cannot weather even the smallest storms. When they get into the slightest battle, they collapse into a whimpering mass of jelly. How can they stand against the enemy like that?

They cannot. So the enemy spreads them on toast and eats them for breakfast. We must be willing to change and grow!

LOVE CONFRONTS

Some people have the idea that the love of God never deals with things. But the love of God is not a nonchalant force. It is a direct, confrontational force that reveals right and wrong because no evil shall be found in the presence of God.

The first thing God did in creation was separate light from darkness. God's love confronts wrong things in our lives so we can recognize them and choose to change. We have to choose to change because God will not do anything against our will.

And they [Jesus and the disciples] come to Jerusalem: and Jesus went into the temple, and began to cast out them that sold and bought in the temple, and overthrew the tables of the moneychangers, and the seats of them that sold doves;

And would not suffer that any man should carry any vessel through the temple.

And he taught, saying unto them, Is it not written, My house shall be called of all nations the house of prayer? but ye have made it a den of thieves.

And the scribes and chief priests heard it, and sought how they might destroy him: for they feared him, because all the people was astonished at his doctrine.

And when even was come, he went out of the city.

Mark 11:15-19 (author's insert)

When Jesus walked into the Temple, His spirit rose up strong and went after those who had begun to make a mockery of the Temple. He physically threw them out. No wimp would have been able to do that! Was He walking in love when He did it? Absolutely! The love in Him confronted the wrong in the Temple; then He taught them what was right.

The same thing applies to us as individuals and as the Church.

Know ye not that ye are the temple of God, and that the Spirit of God dwelleth in you?

1 Corinthians 3:16

We are the temple of the Holy Spirit, and the love of God will confront the wrong things in us and teach us the right things. Now you might say, "Those people's hearts were right. It was not nice for Jesus to toss them out on their ears." However, your heart can be right and your actions be totally wrong. God deals with both. The fact that you have a nice heart does not mean God will let your actions continue to be wrong. He wants both of them conformed to His image.

Confrontation can be taken one of four ways:

• Some people will completely reject the truth of the confrontation and be like the scribes and priests who wanted to kill Jesus for cleaning out the Temple.

• Others will accept the truth of the confrontation but try to avoid any real changes by making excuses. "You don't know what I've been through in my life." Quit finding excuses for your flesh!

• Some will blame the devil for their behavior. It is important to know the difference between what is your own soul and what is demonic influence. If you can choose to continue or discontinue the behavior, then more than likely it is coming from your flesh. However, if the problem or the attitude is hardened and even verges on dogmatism, obsession, or compulsion — perhaps you are being influenced by a demon. Either way you need to rise up in your God-given authority and let your spirit rule. Just say, "From this day forward, I will do it God's way, in Jesus' name." Then don't accept anything less!

• The right way to deal with confrontation is to accept truth and change. There may not be an immediate change, but at least there should be a strong commitment to change. That will get you on the right track. Some things can be changed instantly; others take time.

I know the world needs love, but I believe it needs *godly, tough love.* That is the love that will go out in the ditch and pull you out. It is not the *nice love* that says, "I don't want to get dirty. God, send someone else." Tough love will lift you up out of a mess, sit you down, and show you where you need to change. Then it will help you change.

The Holy Spirit's perfect way of confronting problems in us is by the inward witness. He will continue trying to reach us through the inward witness until we change or become dull of hearing in our hearts. Then I believe He will bring someone to us — an outside voice — to make a very strong impression on our spirits or our souls.

When you are dull of hearing or dull of seeing and the Holy Spirit must bring an outside pressure, the obedient person who talks to you may not know what he is doing. I have had that happen to me several times. Someone would say something to me, and it would prick my heart. They would not know it, but I would think, *Hey, God is trying to get my attention. I better listen here.*

TRUTH OFFENDS SOULISH PEOPLE

Walking in the Spirit keeps you from being offended by the truth of God's Word. If you are walking in the soul, you probably will be offended many times when the truth comes.

> **Then spake Jesus again unto them, saying, I am the light of the world: he that followeth me shall not walk in darkness, but shall have the light of life.**
>
> **The Pharisees therefore said unto him, Thou bearest record of thyself; thy record is not true.**
>
> John 8:12-13

The religious leaders of Jesus' time had a difficult time accepting the truth from Him. The Pharisees said Jesus was lying. He continued to speak the truth to them, and they continued to challenge it. They could not understand it.

Then said Jesus again unto them, I go my way, and ye shall seek me, and shall die in your sins: whither I go, ye cannot come.

Then said the Jews, Will he kill himself? because he saith, Whither I go, ye cannot come.

And he said unto them, Ye are from beneath; I am from above: ye are of this world; I am not of this world.

I said therefore unto you, that ye shall die in your sins: for if ye believe not that I am he, ye shall die in your sins.

Then said they unto him, Who art thou? And Jesus saith unto them, Even the same that I said unto you from the beginning.

I have many things to say and to judge of you: but he that sent me is true; and I speak to the world those things which I have heard of him.

They understood not that he spake to them of the Father.

John 8:21-27

When the truth comes, the soulish person throws up strong defenses to deflect it or misunderstand it because the soul hates to change. The soul will deny the truth and challenge the one who delivers it by saying, "Who do you think you are to be correcting me? What right do you have to say that? Who made you judge over me?"

The soulish walls of the religious leaders were high and thick, but Jesus kept hitting them with the truth, hoping something would finally get through their defenses and prick their hearts so they would repent.

> But now ye seek to kill me, a man that hath told you the truth, which I have heard of God: this did not Abraham.
>
> Ye do the deeds of your father. Then said they to him, We be not born of fornication; we have one Father, even God.
>
> Jesus said unto them, If God were your Father, ye would love me: for I proceeded forth and came from God; neither came I of myself, but he sent me.
>
> Why do you not understand my speech? even because ye cannot hear my word.
>
> Ye are of your father the devil, and the lusts of your father ye will do. He was a murderer from the beginning, and abode not in the truth, because there is no truth in him. When he speaketh a lie, he speaketh of his own: for he is a liar, and the father of it.
>
> And because I tell you the truth, ye believe me not.
>
> John 8:40-45

Jesus confronted them with bold, direct, and hard-hitting words. There were no political or diplomatic words spoken. He did not say, "What you're doing reminds me of a little story...." He knew that when soulish walls are firmly in place, a hint will not do. Only a bold, frontal attack can break through the hardness of the heart and the deafness of the ears.

A friend once told me, "There are so many roots in people's lives that are not of God. It takes bold words and confrontational people to knock those roots out of people, so they can get re-rooted in the Word and produce good fruit."

What kinds of roots are we talking about? Roots of pride, rejection, fear, rebellion, self-will, bitterness, and offense — the list can go on and on. It often takes a bold, anointed word coming from the heart of God to go, "BAM," and destroy those roots.

JEREMIAH – THE CONFRONTATIONAL PROPHET

The prophet Jeremiah was anointed to confront problems and root them out.

> **But the Lord said unto me, Say not, I am a child: for thou shalt go to all that I shall send thee, and whatsoever I command thee thou shalt speak.**
>
> **Be not afraid of their faces: for I am with thee to deliver thee, saith the Lord.**
>
> **Then the Lord put forth his hand, and touched my mouth. And the Lord said unto me, Behold, I have put my words in thy mouth.**
>
> **See, I have this day set thee over the nations and over the kingdoms, to root out, and to pull down, and to destroy, and to throw down, to build, and to plant.**
>
> Jeremiah 1:7-10

Everything in that last verse is a forward push. It takes confrontation to root out, pull down, and destroy. It also takes confrontation to build and plant. The key to the strength of Jeremiah's ministry is in verse 9: *The words of the Lord were in his mouth.* God's confrontation roots out and plants. It pulls out the wrong and plants the right. But confrontation without the Word of the Lord and without His prompting and direction destroys without building up. We must be led by the Spirit in all we say and do.

Woe be unto the pastors that destroy and scatter the sheep of my pasture! saith the Lord.

Therefore thus saith the Lord God of Israel against the pastors that feed my people; Ye have scattered my flock, and driven them away, and have not visited them: behold, I will visit upon you the evil of your doings, saith the Lord.

And I will gather the remnant of my flock out of all countries whither I have driven them, and will bring them again to their folds; and they shall be fruitful and increase.

And I will set up shepherds over them which shall feed them: and they shall fear no more, nor be dismayed, neither shall they be lacking, saith the Lord.

Jeremiah 23:1-4

Jeremiah confronted the problems in Israel that are similar to the problems in the Church today. God was using him to confront the pastors who were hirelings instead of shepherds. Pastors who fail to feed and protect the flocks entrusted to them by God will be removed and replaced by those who will be obedient. We are seeing it today. God will not allow the sheep to be fleeced and scattered anymore.

Spiritual leaders must be led by the Spirit. A pastor who confronts his flock out of his soul instead of his Spirit will destroy them and scatter them. However, a pastor who walks in love and confronts when and how God says to confront will root out and plant. God will bless that pastor. We must know when to confront and when not to. Failing to confront when God says to do so will also hurt the flock.

If God is trying to clean up problems in a church and the leaders are going around saying, "Everything is fine. There are no problems here. Peace and blessings on everyone," those leaders are creating a false sense of security in the flock. A flock will not change, grow, or mature under those circumstances. Those leaders are standing in the way of God's move instead of flowing with it in obedience.

Mine heart within me is broken because of the prophets; all my bones shake; I am like a drunken man, and like a man whom wine hath overcome, because of the Lord, and because of the words of his holiness.

For the land is full of adulterers; for because of swearing the land mourneth; the pleasant places of the wilderness are dried up, and their course is evil, and their force is not right.

For both prophet and priest are profane; yea, in my house have I found their wickedness, saith the Lord.

Wherefore their way shall be unto them as slippery ways in the darkness: they shall be driven on, and fall

therein: for I will bring evil upon them, even the year of their visitation, saith the Lord.

And I have seen folly in the prophets of Samaria; they prophesied in Baal, and caused my people Israel to err.

I have seen also in the prophets of Jerusalem an horrible thing: they commit adultery, and walk in lies: they strengthen also the hands of evildoers, that none doth return from his wickedness: they are all of them unto me as Sodom, and the inhabitants thereof as Gomorrah.

Therefore thus saith the Lord of hosts concerning the prophets; Behold, I will feed them with wormwood, and make them drink the water of gall: for from the prophets of Jerusalem is profaneness gone forth into all the land.

Thus saith the Lord of hosts, Hearken not unto the words of the prophets that prophesy unto you: they make you vain: they speak a vision of their own heart, and not out of the mouth of the Lord.

They say still unto them that despise me, The Lord hath said, Ye shall have peace; and they say unto every one that walketh after the imagination of his own heart, No evil shall come upon you.

For who hath stood in the counsel of the Lord, and hath perceived and heard his word? who hath marked his word, and heard it?

Behold, a whirlwind of the Lord is gone forth in fury, even a grievous whirlwind: it shall fall grievously upon the head of the wicked.

The anger of the Lord shall not return, until he have executed, and till he have performed the thoughts of his heart: in the latter days ye shall consider it perfectly.

I have not sent these prophets, yet they ran: I have not spoken to them, yet they prophesied.

But if they had stood in my counsel, and had caused my people to hear my words, then they should have turned them from their evil way, and from the evil of their doings.

Jeremiah 23:9-22

Jeremiah was confronting the disobedient prophets and priests. God wanted holiness and obedience in Jeremiah's day, and He wants it now! The people will turn from their evil ways if spiritual leaders will listen to the Word of the Lord and speak it forth.

PAUL'S EXAMPLE

The apostle Paul regularly confronted the wrong in the churches through his epistles and in person. He also confronted the other leaders when it was necessary.

But when Peter was come to Antioch, I withstood him to the face, because he was to be blamed.

For before that certain came from James, he did eat with the Gentiles: but when they were come, he withdrew and separated himself, fearing them which were of the circumcision.

And the other Jews dissembled likewise with him; insomuch that Barnabas also was carried away with their dissimulation.

But when I saw that they walked not uprightly according to the truth of the gospel, I said unto Peter before them all, If thou, being a Jew, livest after the manner of Gentiles, and not as do the Jews, why compellest thou the Gentiles to live as do the Jews?

We who are Jews by nature, and not sinners of the Gentiles,

Knowing that a man is not justified by the works of the law, but by the faith of Jesus Christ, even we have believed in Jesus Christ, that we might be justified by the faith of Christ, and not by the works of the law: for by the works of the law shall no flesh be justified.

Galatians 2:11-16

Paul confronted Peter face to face. He did not backbite and grumble about him behind his back. He boldly confronted the wrong so Peter and the others could grow and change.

Confrontation is a major part of the new move of God because holiness will not come without it. We have been able to get away with certain things in the past but not in this new move. Jesus is looking for a bride without spot or wrinkle, and we will never get to that place unless we confront the unholiness in our lives and get it out. We must bring every area of life into absolute obedience to God and His Word.

CHAPTER 9

THE CHURCH MUST
WALK IN AUTHORITY

Authority must come back into the pulpits of America, not *soulish strength*, but *spiritual authority*. We have begun to see the strength of God come forth in those who are walking by the Spirit and living in the authority and the command of God. Those who are concerned about everyone else's opinions will not walk in spiritual authority.

Devils hate authority. They love soulish talk and religious talk because there is no real authority being exercised over them. However, when someone knows their authority in God, they squirm. When Jesus went to a synagogue in Capernaum one Saturday during the Sabbath service, His authority caused a demon to get stirred up.

> **And they were astonished at his doctrine: for he taught them as one that had authority, and not as the scribes.**

And there was in their synagogue a man with an unclean spirit; and he cried out,

Saying, Let us alone; what have we to do with thee, thou Jesus of Nazareth? art thou come to destroy us? I know thee who thou art, the Holy One of God.

And Jesus rebuked him, saying, Hold thy peace, and come out of him.

Mark 1:22-25

How God anointed Jesus of Nazareth with the Holy Ghost and with power: who went about doing good, and healing all that were oppressed of the devil; for God was with him.

Acts 10:38

Healing and deliverance go hand in hand. There is coming a great surge of deliverance. I believe that before we hit the end-time revival, there will be a cleanup time in order for the glorious Church to become glorious. One way to get cleaned up is through deliverance. The end-time revival will not be a deliverance revival, but deliverance will be part of it. I also feel there will come a time, as we move into the greater glory of God, when there will be reactions to that glory. Demons on people in the services will manifest. So what do you do? You take care of them and go on. You do not exalt deliverance; you exalt the Deliverer.

MANY THINGS WILL BE REVEALED

The Spirit is being poured out on all flesh in a greater portion. Do you know what happens when the Holy Spirit hits flesh?

Whatever is in that person will react to the Spirit. If God is strong in them, they will react positively to the presence of God. If a demon is controlling them, they will react with resistance.

Every church needs to allow the voice of God to come to them again in deliverance. People called into healing ministries who do not want to cast out devils will not see the magnitude of what their ministries could be. Strong healing and strong deliverance should be a way of life to any minister who wants to be part of what God is doing.

You do not wash devils by the Word — you cast them out. You wash the individual. Devils are not going to be cleansed. Some of them will leave through the preaching of the Word, but what we are facing in the harvest coming into the Church is a great need for deliverance.

We are dealing with a class of devils who plan their strategy and wait for the ideal time to cause a person to fall. Then the demon will try to hinder that person in the future through the memory of that fall. I believe God is raising up a new breed of minister — and a new breed of believer — who will blast these devils out of the Church!

Believers are being raised up with anointings to take cities and nations, not just one block. However, if these territories are not taken through deliverance, they will rise and fall because they will not be able to live on track with God. The devil is trying to put them in bondage and break them, but Jesus wants them free.

HOMELIFE IS OF GREAT IMPORTANCE

From my study of great men and women of God in the past, I have learned that their home lives were of major importance. Devils go after children because they are vulnerable. If parents do not provide spiritual protection and covering, children are more vulnerable.

I was raised in a very godly and powerful home. There were many things common to my home that I found later were not common in other people's homes. One was fighting the devil. I could walk home from school, come in the front door, and if something was not right, my parents or my grandparents would grab me and cast that spirit off. After that I was fine.

PENTECOSTAL-CHARISMATIC WITCHCRAFT

Another problem today is what I call "pentecostal-charismatic witchcraft." That involves people who love the Lord in Full Gospel churches, but who are not in the realm of the Holy Spirit. They get out there in the soul and end up running around with familiar spirits and having visions that do not come from heaven. The Church must learn to deal with this in bold and plain ways.

In these cases, a pastor should not say, "Let's pray for them." He should get that spirit off them so they can be free from bondage. Also, I want you to be aware that people in the fivefold offices are not immune to soulish operations or demonic influence:

- A pastor who gets in the flesh becomes someone who strives to control his sheep.
- An evangelist who gets in the flesh goes "Hollywood."
- A teacher who gets in the flesh simply gives out information with no anointing and can become critical of other people who do not say things exactly the same way.
- A prophet who gets in the flesh gets spacey or judgmental.
- An apostle who gets in the flesh gets legalistic and prideful.

BEWARE OF FALSE GIFTS

Maria Woodworth-Etter, the well-known evangelist from the turn of the century, said, "At the same time God gives me a gift of the Holy Spirit, the devil tries to give me a false one."

I believe the operations of the prophet and apostle are going to be revealed in greater authority than we have ever seen before. We will see things pulled down, destroyed, and thrown away. The proper building and planting will be done. Ideas of devils and men will be blasted away.

Musicians and singers will operate in a deeper dimension of the Spirit as well as the fivefold offices. God is invading every part of our lives and ministries, and He wants to rearrange the music departments of our churches. No longer can we get by with singing the standard three songs on Sunday morning and be done for the week. To experience God's glory, we must enter His gates with thanksgiving and His courts with praise. (See Psalm 100:4.)

We have lost great musicians and singers to the secular music industry because we would not instruct them or because they would not receive instruction. Even musicians and singers need to learn discernment because with a special anointing comes responsibility. Many people want the glory, but they do not want the responsibility. The responsibility of the power and the glory is great. It is not a game!

One of the greatest reasons people get into error is that if they lose the real anointing, they reach out and get a false one. Just because someone produces signs and wonders does not always mean it is from God. If my spirit witnesses something wrong with a minister, yet there are still miracles taking place, I will not go near that person. I have sense enough to go by my spirit and not my head.

The Church must wake up to the presence of the demonic world because in the days to come there will be the false anointed as well as the real anointed performing signs and wonders. You cannot go by what you see, and Christians need to be careful.

STAY WHERE GOD PUTS YOU

One reason so many people have not been able to grow spiritually is because they do not stay in one church long enough to get what God wants them to get. They run to this seminar to see a special speaker, or they run to hear someone prophesy somewhere else. And they keep running. God will be patient for a while, but eventually, those who run every which way will lose their joy. God has placed the cloud of the Spirit on the church He has called them to — but they are not there! He has given gifts to prophesy, heal, and deliver — but they missed them!

Quit being a "church hopper" if that is what you have been doing. Find out where God wants you to be and stay there, regardless of circumstances. Don't be deceived by running to and fro.

HOLINESS IS REQUIRED TODAY

I believe that in this next move of God, you will need to live a life of holiness to get blessed. You cannot keep sinning on Saturday nights and expect to be blessed on Sunday mornings. When the devil throws sinful thoughts at you, you must cast them down. God wants us to live in His righteousness and holiness every moment of every day.

For I am the Lord your God: ye shall therefore sanctify yourselves, and ye shall be holy; for I am holy: neither shall ye defile yourselves with any manner of creeping thing that creepeth upon the earth.

For I am the Lord that bringeth you up out of the land of Egypt, to be your God: ye shall therefore be holy, for I am holy.

Leviticus 11:44-45

If God required holiness in the days written of in the book of Acts, He requires it today. If He required holiness in the early days of the creation of the world, He requires it today. No matter what generation you are of or how you were raised, when God says something, it is so. When He says we must live holy, then we better be living holy!

Holiness is so important. If you do not live holy, you will not live long in God's glory. We need the Word of God coming from the mouths of His ministers with such holiness that it will cause action in the pews.

HOLY VESSELS

I beseech you therefore, brethren, by the mercies of God, that ye present your bodies a living sacrifice, holy, acceptable unto God, which is your reasonable service.

And be not conformed to this world: but be ye transformed by the renewing of your mind, that ye may prove what is that good, and acceptable, and perfect, will of God.

Romans 12:1-2

I believe we are going to see a great coming together in the body of Christ because unity in the Church brings the atmosphere in which the Holy Spirit feels welcome and comfortable. We must build an environment where He likes to dwell. We must keep it clean from devils and clean from the flesh. We must get in the world of the Holy Spirit and learn to operate as the Holy Spirit directs.

A good environment is one that is cleansed of the world, the flesh, and the devil. A good environment now will save you much trouble and pain later. It can keep you from falling. Many ministers who believe in deliverance today have the idea that a good environment is one where demons come out nicely and quietly. That is not the case. This new move of God is a move of action, not discussion. A good environment is one where demons come out and leave — period — and they are never allowed to return!

Most people do not want demons to holler when they come out. Some believe that if demons holler, then the one doing the deliverance is not spiritually strong. If you read the New Testament, you will see that demons cast out by Jesus yelled on their way out. And if He experienced it in His ministry, we can certainly expect to experience it in ours.

In the Garden of Eden, Adam and Eve realized they were naked and hid when God came asking, "Where are you?" Today, God is still coming and asking ministers, "Where are you?" And many of them are not where they are supposed to be! Many are not wearing their spiritual clothing. They are not operating in God's anointing.

If you do not have God's fresh anointing, you do not have on your spiritual clothing. That means it is time to get your environment straightened out so you can walk in boldness and holiness.

EXERCISE AUTHORITY IN BOLDNESS

It is time to invade the devil's territory. Do not be ashamed of the Gospel. Do not be ashamed of the revelations God gives you. If you make a mistake, admit it, ask everyone to forgive you, and go on. Take your God-given authority and use it.

If a pastor turns a church service over to me, it is my responsibility to keep things in order. If people begin to do things that are not right, it is up to me to exercise authority and deal with it.

Pastors, if demons begin to act up in your service, take your God-given, Jesus-delegated authority and cast them out. You must learn to walk in authority and not feel guilty. I had to learn how to look at people and tell them to stop because what they were doing was not right. I had to learn to tell them to sit down and not feel guilty about it. Exercising spiritual authority is not domination, however. We are not to dominate our congregations — that's the Holy Spirit's job. But when situations and circumstances arise that are not of God, it is the pastor's job to put a stop to it. Otherwise, other people in the church are affected and effective ministry cannot continue.

You need to become ruthless in your faith to become an invading force. The spirit world needs to know who you are in Christ. Be brave in your faith, stir up the gift of God that is within you, and walk in holy boldness.

If the world ever needed healing and deliverance ministries, it needs them now!

If the Church ever needed healing and deliverance ministries, it needs them now!

CONCLUSION

God is cleansing His Church. He wants a spotless and clean Church, one without sin. This is not just so believers will feel better, either! It is because God has a plan.

God's plan is that nations will be changed and cities will become places of spiritual greatness — not of perversion. He has places in the country that are no longer "nice teaching centers," but are becoming militant schools to train soldiers of the Cross. Soldiers are being sent out to blast the devil, to establish truth, and to make the name of the Lord be the salvation of the cities and towns where they are.

It is exciting to be a part of God's plan! This is the day when all things shall come to pass. Another word of the Lord came to me for the Church that pertains to this time:

Rearrangements are coming to the righteous people of the earth — rearrangements of lifestyles and goals. Plans that have been made shall be altered, saith the Spirit of the Lord.

They have planned to move this way and to function that way, but My plan shall interrupt their plans and rearrangements shall come even of the anointings that they carry at this hour. The anointings in which many have grown comfortable shall no longer produce for them as they have in the past. I have a fresh plan, a fresh power, and a fresh anointing for all who are of My name. But they must realize it, accept it, and begin to flow in it in a very zealous way.

This is the day when the way in which the youth flow also shall be arranged. Many of them have planned for this and for that, but their learning shall speed up and the growth of their inner man also shall speed up. They shall be young, yet old. They will stand in positions of authority and lead masses while the age of the bodies in which they live are yet young.

Marriages shall take on a new look and a new flow. The way children are trained in the home also will be different. No longer will children be just nice little boys or girls who play with toys, but they shall be children who also pray and sing and do the work of the Lord while they are yet young.

Many say, "I want to run this way" (be a part of what God is doing), but there are things that bind them and weigh them down. But there has come a time when such things will be broken. Weights and anchors will fall. Men's minds will become pure again. Men's hearts will become strong, beating with the Gospel way.

The young and the old shall flow together as one. There will not be two individual camps, but there shall be one.

And there shall be rearrangements of desires inside many. This is the day when I will make even those crooked places straight, says the Lord. I will cause the desires of the hearts and of the flesh to come out in the right (alignment). Things you know are wrong, yet cannot seem to do anything about, the Spirit of the Lord will come upon, correct, rearrange, readjust, and heal those things that need to be taken care of.

Do you want to be a part of God's revival? Or do you want to just stay in the old? Now is the time to make your choice. The hour of God has dawned. Be a part — do your part, and God will do His part. It's time to *Run to the Battle!*

ABOUT THE AUTHOR

Blessed with a gift of unusually strong preaching, Roberts Liardon has answered a worldwide calling of God which came to him when he was an eight-year-old boy. Having preached in 93 nations, Roberts Liardon is founder and senior pastor of Embassy Christian Center and Spirit Life Bible College and was twice elected the Most Outstanding Young Man in America.

A best-selling author, Roberts' books have been translated into over 33 languages, and his audio and video tapes have helped strengthen and change the body of Christ all over the world.

ROBERTS LIARDON MINISTRIES
INTERNATIONAL OFFICES:

EUROPE
Roberts Liardon Ministries
7 Stirling Way
Welwyn Garden City
Herts AL72QA
England
Phone and Fax: 44 1707 327 222

SOUTH AFRICA
Roberts Liardon Ministries
P. O. Box 3155
Kimberley 8300
South Africa
Phone and Fax: 2753 832 1207

AUSTRALIA
Roberts Liardon Ministries
P. O. Box 7
Kingsgrove NSW 1480
Australia
Phone and Fax: 011 61 500 555056

USA
Roberts Liardon Ministries
P. O. Box 30710
Laguna Hills, California 92654
Phone: (949) 833-3555
Fax: (949) 833-9555

or
www.robertsliardon.org

Seven reasons you should attend Spirit Life Bible College

1. SLBC is a **spiritual school** with an academic support; not an academic school with a spiritual touch.

2. SLBC teachers are **successful ministers** in their own right. Pastor Roberts Liardon will not allow failure to be imparted into his students.

3. SLBC is a member of **Oral Roberts University Educational Fellowship** and is fully **accredited** with the International Christian Accrediting Association.

4. SLBC hosts monthly seminars with some of the **world's greatest** ministers who add another element, anointing, and impartation to the students' lives.

5. Roberts Liardon understands your commitment to come to SLBC and commits himself to students by **ministering weekly** in classroom settings.

6. SLBC provides **hands-on** ministerial training.

7. SLBC provides ministry opportunity through its **post-graduate placement program**.

-------------------------- CLIP ALONG LINE & MAIL TO ROBERTS LIARDON MINISTRIES. --------------------------

Spirit Life Partner

Wouldn't It Be Great...

- If you could send 500 missionaries to the nations of the earth?
- If you could travel 250,000 air miles, boldly preaching the Word of God in 93 nations?
- If you could strengthen and train the next generation of God's leaders?
- If you could translate 27 books and distribute them into 37 countries?

Project Joseph Food Outreach.

...Now You Can!

Maybe you can't go, but by supporting this ministry every month, your gift can help to communicate the Gospel around the world.

-------------------- ✂ CLIP ALONG LINE & MAIL TO ROBERTS LIARDON MINISTRIES. --------------------

☐ **YES!!** Pastor Roberts, I want to support your work in the kingdom of God by becoming a **SPIRIT LIFE PARTNER.** Please find enclosed my first monthly gift.

Name_____

Address_____

City_____ State_____ Zip_____

Phone (_____) _____

SPIRIT LIFE PARTNER AMOUNT: $_____

☐ Check / Money Order ☐ VISA ☐ American Express ☐ Discover ☐ MasterCard

☐☐☐☐ ☐☐☐☐ ☐☐☐☐ ☐☐☐☐

Name On Card_____ Exp. Date___/___/___

Signature_____ Date___/___/___

Roberts Liardon Ministries

P.O. Box 30710 ♦ Laguna Hills, CA 92654 ♦ (949) 833-3555 ♦ Fax (949) 833.9555 ♦ www.robertsliardon.org

BOOKS BY ROBERTS LIARDON

Run to the Battle
(A Compiliation of *The Invading Force,*
A Call to Action, and *Run to the Battle*)

John G. Lake:
The Complete Collection of His Life Teachings

Breaking Controlling Powers

Smith Wigglesworth Speaks to Students of the Bible

Sharpen Your Discernment

Smith Wigglesworth:
The Complete Collection of His Life Teachings

God's Generals

God's Generals Workbook

Cry of the Spirit:
Unpublished Sermons by Smith Wigglesworth

Forget Not His Benefits

Haunted Houses, Ghosts & Demons

Holding to the Word of the Lord

I Saw Heaven

Kathryn Kuhlman:
A Spiritual Biography of God's Miracle-Working Power

Religious Politics

School of the Spirit

Spiritual Timing

The Price of Spiritual Power

The Quest for Spiritual Hunger

Also Available:

God's Generals Video Collection
(12 Video Tapes)

Additional copies of this book and other book titles
from ALBURY PUBLISHING are
available at your local bookstore.

ALBURY PUBLISHING
P. O. Box 470406
Tulsa, Oklahoma 74147-0406

For a complete list of our titles,
visit us at our web site:
www.alburypublishing.com

For international and Canadian orders,
please contact:

Access Sales International
2448 East 81st Street
Suite 4900
Tulsa, Oklahoma 74137
Phone 918-523-5590 Fax 918-496-2822